HORSE NONSENSE

D1350195

By the Same Authors

1066 AND ALL THAT
AND NOW ALL THIS
GARDEN RUBBISH AND OTHER
COUNTRY BUMPS

THE BEST PEOPLE

HORSE NONSENSE

BY THE AUTHORS AND THE ARTIST OF
1066 AND ALL THAT

CONSISTING OF PICTURES BY

JOHN REYNOLDS
(VICEMASTER, BLOOMSBURY DRUGHOUNDS)

AND TEXT BY

R. J. YEATMAN
(EX-TEMP: GENT: R.F.A.)

IN COLLABORATION WITH

W. C. SELLAR
(EX-SECRET-MEMBER BERWICKSHIRE F.H.)

METHUEN

Published by Methuen 1999

1 3 5 7 9 10 8 6 4 2

First published in the United Kingdom in 1933
by Methuen & Co Ltd

This edition published in 1999 by
Methuen Publishing Limited
215 Vauxhall Bridge Road, London SW1V 1EJ

Peribo Pty Ltd, 58 Beaumont Road, Mount Kuring-Gai
NSW 2080, Australia, ACN 002 273 761
(for Australia and New Zealand)

Copyright © 1933 by W.C. Sellar and R.J. Yeatman

Methuen Publishing Limited Reg. No. 3543167

A CIP catalogue record for this book
is available from the British Library

ISBN 0 413 73990 2

Printed and bound in the United Kingdom by
Cox & Wyman Ltd, Reading, Berkshire

This book is sold subject to the condition that it shall not,
by way of trade or otherwise, be lent, resold, hired out, or
otherwise circulated without the publisher's prior consent in any
form of binding or cover other than that in which it is published
and without a similar condition including this condition being
imposed on the subsequent purchaser.

Papers used by Methuen Publishing Limited are natural,
recyclable products made from wood grown in sustainable
forests. The manufacturing processes conform to environmental
regulations of the country of origin.

CONTENTS

BIT I
THE NOBLE ART

BIT II
THE NOBLE ANIMAL

BIT III
BUYING IT

BIT IV
RIDING IT

HORSE NONSENSE

Bit V
THE HORSE AT HOME

Bit VI
HUNTING ON THE HORSE

Bit VII
PUNTING ON THE HORSE

Bit VIII
THE HORSE IN HISTORY AND LITERATURE

Bit IX
DRIVING IT

BIBLIOGRAPHY

PRESS OPINIONS OF THIS BOOK

Col. F. le Ch. Numnah-Smith, M.F.H., V.C., etc. etc., author of *The Noble Animal*, etc. etc., writing in *The White Man's Magazine* :—

'Drivelling bosh . . . ill-bred . . . horse is always right . . . my life in the saddle . . . Melton Mowbray . . . The Chestnut Troop . . . Poona . . . '86, '96, '06, my Bay Gelding . . . my Books . . . my Ancestors . . . 1066 . . . Whyte Melville . . . Lindsay Gordon . . . Beckford . . . Surtees . . . This contemptible book . . . not even gentlemen . . . horsewhipped . . .

. . . .

Capt. W. D. Pontoon, M.C., R.E., author of *Dirigible Quadrupeds*, etc., writing in *The Transport Review* :—

' Joking astride . . . very reasonable book . . . horse never intelligent . . . mule (and femule) better all round . . . my own Book . . . Mechanisation . . . Forward Seat . . . Square on the hypotenuse . . . Moment of Inertia . . . Eohippos. . . Nejdi . . . Napoleon . . . Stone Walls . . . Tom Walls . . . Tom Mix . . . Tom Webster . . . Tom Cobley and All Those . . .

HORSE NONSENSE

BIT I

THE NOBLE ART

CHAPTER I

HIPPOCRACY OR THE IMPORTANCE OF BEING HORSE-CONSCIOUS

'He doth nothing but talk of his Horse.'
SHAKESPEARE, *Merchant of Venice.*

'Bad about the Horse—it's simply frumptious
to be Bad about the Horse.'
FOËL COWARD.

TO confess that you are totally Ignorant about the Horse, is social suicide : you will be despised by everybody, especially the horse. In decent society (see rather decent picture above) you will be spurned, or even spurred, aside as a *pariah*.

Indecent Society (regardez rather indecent picture below) will be your only refuge. . . .

It has always been so. The Best People have always been obsequiously horse-conscious (a case of Rank Hippocracy, asyermightsay).

For example, Archæologists (asyermayn'tknow) declare that the prehistoric Man-About-The-Downs actually worshipped the Horse (provided it was a *pukkah* White Horse).

The Ancient Romans were horse-bitten, too. Whom did Julius Cæsar elect (after consulting the auspices) to throw across your old friend the River Flumen? Not the *Infantry* (mere conscript fathers, nondescript uncles, etc.) but the *Cavalry*, or *Equites*, all of whom had to prove that they were ablative absolute gents and ' as rich as Creosote ' (to use the old Roman Army slang).

Again, what is Polo ? *Ans :* Polo is a species of horse-croquet invented by the Lofty Maharajahs of India, or possibly the Shifty Shaherezadjahs of Perzhia, or possibly by the Chinese during the p'ing p'ong dynasty—we don't know—but the point is, Polo has always been the only exclusively aristocratic pastime, limited to the Best People (*chukkah-sahibs* and all those) and played most exclusively at the other end of the ground, so that the Common People shall never comprehend it.

In short, if you were cordially invited, by Mr. C. B. Cochran, say, to depict *The Best People Through the Ages*—what would be the Right Answer ? *Rt. Hon. Ans :* A CAVALCADE, featuring *Knights* of Olde Englande, *Chevaliers* d'Old France, *Caballeros* of Old Spain (word still displayed at suitable spots on Dos

Old Spanish Rlys), Sheikhs of Araby, Ironsides and
Cavaliers, Highwaymen and Hunting Squires, Jockeys
and Joint-Masters and similar Pomponious Egoes (*see
Frontispiece*). All mounted, all Horsemen ; not one
hiker amongst 'em.

     .   .   .   .   .   .

It is the same to-day. The Best People are still
horse-conscious—neigh, animal-minded. In their eyes,
persons who betray Blank Ignorance of The Horse,
or, worse still, downright brutish Indifference to The
Noble Animal, are definitely *beyond the pail.*

As for you, reader, if you go on like that, you will be
written down as a Congenital Pedestrian, an Hereditary
Hobbledyhike. D*mmitsir ! In the end, you won't—
even in print we can only whisper it—*you won't even be sure
you're a g*ntl*m*n. . . .*

CHAPTER II

IN WHICH THE WHOLE ART OF HORSEMANSHIP
IS GRADUALLY EXPLODED

> ' He who doesn't know
> And lets you know he doesn't know
> Is a *Cad.*
> *Throat-lash him.*'
>
> Old Arab Proverb

Do not, however, be personally alarmed. You, Sir,
(this is from the horse's mouth) are personally quite
all right. Especially if you are English : because the
English are not only born Statesmen, Seamen, Policemen and experts at poking the fire, but also the only

Despised by everybody

Born Horsemen in the world. As Col: Numnah-Smith[1] says in his stupendous book *The Noble Animal* (pp. 6, 17, 38 and 416), ' It is their birthright and their right.'

Even if you are not English (bad luck, sir !)—even if you are Scotch (well tried !), or Erse, or Worse, you are still all right ; since anyone, by reading the following chapters and studying the diagrams, etc., can rapidly acquire a thorough-going mastery of *The True Art of Horsemanship*. As for being Erse, everyone knows that all Irishmen are not only Curragh-going Horsemen, but thurragh-going horse-copers into the bargain (Hurragh !).

*   *   *

What then is this famous Art of Horsemanship, at which the Best People have always excelled themselves —which gives them the whip-hand, and those formidable grip-knees, and enables them to walk as curiously and behave as spuriously as they like, and get away with it all through the Ages ?

The Truth, which we reveal here for the first time (having only just realised it), is this : The Whole Art of Horsemanship consists in knowing How TO TALK ABOUT THE HORSE.

*   *   *

To acquire this Noble Art no sacrifice, obviously, can be too great. So *buy a horse*, by all means, if you think it necessary ; *learn to ride it*—if your indecent Social engagements (see p. 2 again if you like) permit ; learn to *groom* it, and *shoe* it, and *boot* it, and *shoo* it, and *fire* it, and *drench* it, and *d*mmit*, and even *break*

---

[1] Col: F. le Ch. Numnah-Smith, M.F.H., V.C., D.S.O., O.P., etc.

it (to bits, bridles, etc.)—if you have absolutely nothing to do with your time. But remember, *Horsemanship comes first.* If you want to keep your place in the Cavalcade you *must talk about The Horse;* not in a simple footslogging sort of way—that would never do —but using such a wealth of equinoxious terminology that your conversation becomes just one long horse-word puzzle.

For there is nothing truer in literature than the old Arab slogan—

> ' He who Knows,
> And lets you Know he Knows,
> Is a *Horseman,*
> D*mmit.'

BIT II
THE NOBLE ANIMAL

CHAPTER I

POINTS ABOUT THE HORSE

*' I know two things about the Horse
And one of them is rather coarse.'*
H. BELLOC.

THOUGH the Best People usually prefer breeding, riding, etc., to arithmetic, all True Horsemen are aware that The Horse is numerically divided into fore quarters, fifteen or sixteen hands, no fingers, dozens of dirty teeth (Tush, Tush !) and, in addition, a number of infinitely debatable *Points*.

That may surprise you, because at first sight The Animal often appears to have no particular point about it at all (see Fig. I). Except possibly the ears.

This view of the horse, however, is not acceptable to the Best People. On the contrary, in the eyes

Fig. I.—At first sight

of a Horseman, the Horse is a *mass of Points*. Which is the reason why the conversation of horsemen, despite any evidence to the contrary, is never pointless, but moves easily from Point-to-Point (see Figs. II, III, etc.) ; returning often to the point from which it started.

All the points illustrated below are worth mentioning as frequently as possible, so you had better learn them off by heart, unless, of course, a knowledge of The Points of the Horse has been born in you owing to the exceptionally thorough way in which you were bred.

To make it easier for you to do this, we have systematised these points into A. The interlocking system of pointing (Fig. II). B. The Hithers and Blithers system (Fig. III). C. The Umps system (Fig. IV). (See overleaf.)

Of course, there are dozens more of these talking points, but only stud-grooms and other very advanced horsemen are expected to mention all the innumerable locks, socks and barrels, cushions and coronets, and similar mysterious ingredients out of which Nature has miraculously concocted The Horse, and to know when to lock the postern or oil the pistern or fire the cannon-bone and all that.

All a g*ntl*m*n needs is to be able to ' fault ' his friend's horses, i.e. to run his eye knowingly over the noble animals and murmur, ' A little long in the matlock, eh ? ' or ' A little wrong in the padlock, dontyerthink ? ' or ' A trifle inclined to stifle—not a *windjammer*, I trust ? ' Horsemen are generous to a fault, especially in their own animals, so your friend will doubtless point out why these are all just optical illusions, sceptical allusions, and so on. But at least

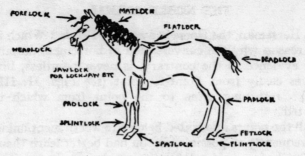

Fig. II.—Interlocking

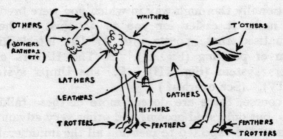

Fig. III.—Hithers and Blithers

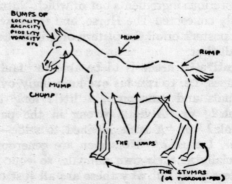

Fig. IV.—Umps

you will have let everybody see what a fatlot you know about it.

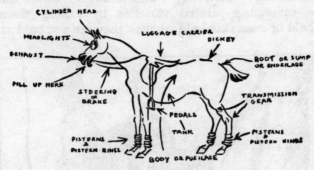

CYLINDER HEAD
HEADLIGHTS
EXHAUST
FILL UP HERE
STEERING OR BRAKE
LUGGAGE CARRIER
DICKEY
BOOT OR SUMP OR ENSILAGE
TRANSMISSION GEAR
PEDALS
TANK
PISTERNS & PISTERN RINGS
BODY OR FUSILAGE
PISTERNS & PISTERN RINGS

Special system of Points for motorists

CHAPTER II

G*NTL*M*N, AND ARTISTS, PREFER GREYS

WOMEN, especially, find exquisite boredom in trying to describe horses by their *colours*. After being rebuked a few times for calling a *blue-roan* horse 'gun-metal', *liver-chestnuts* 'nigger', *duns* 'beige', and *sorrels* 'nude', and so on, they usually give it up, contenting themselves with the knowledge that a dappled or fish-net style is available both in horse and hose.

The fact is, almost any horse is a 'dark horse' when it comes to telling its colour, because it is a code of honour among horsemen to call obviously black horses

' brown ' and obviously brown horses ' light-bay ' or
' chestnut ' and the demonstrably horse-chestnut-
coloured ones ' dark bay ', and finally to insult the
rare camouflage-painted varieties by calling them
piebald or even skewbald (though they are not bald at

Dappled, or fish-net style

all, in fact quite as horsute as the others) : so that the
Common People are bemused by all this equivocation,
and Film Producers give it up and boldly classify all
horses as either *blondes* or *brunettes* (*see opposite*).

The question ' Which is the best colour ? ' exercised
our forefathers a great deal, especially during the
XVIIth Century when whole chapters were written to
decide whether a good horse could have more than
two white legs, etc. ; but in time horsemen decided to
agree on the Rule that ' A Good Horse may be of Any

Colour ' (except green), provided it avoids chintzes, checks and tartans (which accounts, no doubt, for the comparative indifference of Scotsmen to The Noble Animal).

But it is certain that of all colours grey is the most

popular; especially with Artists, who find the tone contrasts so tritely with the vermilion costumes of the Hunt or the scarlet uniform of the Life Guards. (The Lifeguards' horses, however, look rather Black if you mention this—and even if you don't.)

Similarly, in the even more highly coloured stories which hunting men tell themselves after dinner it is always ' the old grey mare ' who so gallantly leapt the gates of the level-crossing *and* a couple of goods-trains (which happened, like the Port, to be trundling by).

In short, you are quite safe in mentioning, both over the port and when you join the ladies, that '*The Grey Mare is the Better Horse.*'

CHAPTER III

SHIRE AND D*M

(Very difficult : cribs may be used, especially by the Horse)

> ' *Ride a Cock-horse*
> *To Handley Cross.*'
> Old Nursery Rhyme.

BESIDES a good repertoire of Points and Colours you must have also at your wits' end plenty of different *kinds of horses* to talk about. It is not very knowing just to mention ' my horse ' : it is much nobler to talk about my *mare, filly, spalding* and so on.

These terms are easy. All horses are born foals, the female adolescents being called ' fillies ', and the males ' sillies '. When they reach 2 years old, horses are called (for some filly reason) ' Two-year-olds '. A mare (hen-horse or hinny), so long as she is youngish and unmarried, is called ' *A Heiffer* ' (pronounced ' heffer ') ; and a grown-up male is either (pronounced eether) ' *A Spalding* ' or else ' *A Bullion* '—the latter being the very dangerous kind with a ring in its nose. Horse-fathers are called ' *shires* ' and horse-mothers ' *d*ms* ' (some of this horse-language is, we agree, rather *soiling*).

But these are not enough ; you must learn as well to discuss Breed and Blood : and the first thing to note is that the most famous and noble Breed of horse is the English Thorough-bred or bloodoss, and that all thoroughbreds are directly bred from the famous Darby Arabian race-horse (by the barbarous Lord

Godolphin or his friend Madrali the Terrible Turk)
and are notable for their long thin legs, manes, tails
and pedigrees.

Next in nobility comes the pure-bred Arab or
' Steed ', which is chiefly useful for poetry and other
romantic writings. The Arab resembles the Bloodoss
closely, except that the Nose or Nuzzle is rather
sharper (for which reason an Arab is sometimes referred
to as a ' Barb '), and the best kind of Arab is usually
a flea-bitten Grey ; and the worst, undoubtedly, a
fly-blown Bey with greasy socks, seedy-toes, etc.

*   *   *

Other breeds worth your mention are *Shetland
Ponies* (deliberately knitted by Providence, according
to ' Nimrod ',[1] in such a way that children can hold
on anywhere, even underneath) ; ' *Whalers* ', a splendid
back-raking horse-bred type of horse from the Ant-
arctic ; and the *Hackney*, *Stepney* or *Putney*, a high-
steppin' breed with hard feet suitable for riding on
the Kerb.

There are also the native *Indian ponies* (or chutneys)
and the North American jitneys, whitneys and chiffney-
bitneys, and finally the several types of *cart-horse*
such as the Clydesiders, the Wensleydales, the Suffolk
Perch, the Rumpuncheon and the Shyer, with which
types, however, a g*ntl*m*n is not much concerned.

Finally there is that splendidly independent self-
made mount, the handy-English-hunter-with-no-dam-
circus-tricks-about-it, which causes plenty of grief and

[1] ' Nimrod ' (Mr. C. J. Apperly) was the first famous gentleman
horse-correspondent ; was born in 1779 ; wrote unceasingly about
The Noble Animal, & Himself, for 30 years ; never refused anything
except a creditor and died (still a gentleman) in 1843.

concern in the hunting field, the Royal Show and even the Royal Family.

*   *   *

A NOTE ON JOINING THE PERCHERON SOCIETY

Cart-horses, besides being useful for giving children rides, whinneying behind hedges, and trotting up and down looking like policemen running, are very clever at getting Societies formed round them. Of these the most exclusive probably is the Percheron Society, which is very difficult to get into as the qualifications are *low shoulders, well-sprung ribs, broad knees with a very little silky hair below, the feet free from indents and cracks and the heels well opened out, no seedy toes, clean legs, short powerful neck and a rather small head rather badly set-on.* Very few people come up to these requirements; but if it so happens that *you do*, then you should undoubtedly apply at once to join the Percheron Society, using the printed form supplied on request.

A NOTE ON SPECIAL BREEDS

> ' The Hobby Horse is Forgot.'
> SHAKESPEARE (twice)

In addition to these normal breeds there are a number of abnormal or special breeds such as *Circus Horses* (with their d*m tricks), including Mathematical Horses (which, however, don't really count); and *Film Horses* which can climb rocks, roofs and rope-ladders, nuzzle heroes, muzzle villains, never kick the Producer or eat the camera, and apparently have 4-leg brakes since they can stop dead when cantering at approximately 100 miles-an-hour; *Vaulting-horses* (the only breed which has adjustable legs and no head); *Rocking-horses* (which are the most closely bred of all types, being always of a dapple-grey colour with curly green rockers); political *Stalking-horses* (under cover of which diplomats skirmish warily up and down the Quai d'Orsay); and the *Common Towel-horse*, which would be a jolly good animal if only the towel would stay mounted.

A SPECIAL BREED

Bunjy-grey Fresh Water-horse or Hippodumpus (Greek: Slippobottomos) discovered and unsuccessfully ridden by the authors at the Grand Caledonian Lido, Moffat, Dumf., N.B. It proved impossible to mount.

BIT III

BUYING IT

CHAPTER I

THE BIG LAUGHS

' " Sporting " is only another word for " fair." '
COL. McTAGGART.

IN the course of the day's run of horse-talk the
question may crop up in your mind : Should I
not (now and then) crack a few well-bred *jokes*
about the Horse ? And if so, can it be done without
trotting out a string of aged chestnuts ?

The answer is, yes and no. A horseman should be
gay at suitable times, as well as a little cavalier at all
times, yet you are right if you suspect that unbridled
jesting about the Noble Animal is not well received in
decent society, and that *you* won't be, either, if you
go in for it.

From this it might appear safer not to give rein to
your sense of humour at all. But as a matter of fact,
it is not quite so bad as that. Indeed, you will find
that the problem of bridled joking about the horse is
much simplified by the fact that there are really *only
two jokes.*

At first you will probably not be able to see either
of the jokes ; but does that matter ? Learn to make
them, first, and remember that ' in Horsemanship
nothing is attained but by precept and practice '
(Col. Numnah-Smith, *The Noble Animal, passim*) : in

time you will learn not only to make the jokes but to
join in the well-bred horse-laugh which invariably
greets either of them, especially when correctly
depicted in a decently humorous Magazine.

The first of these positively fundamental jokes is, of
course, the ' Man ' (heaven help him) who Knows Very
Little About The Horse.   This joke is divided into
two sections, (a) when the Man has a lot of money :
which makes it funnier but unfortunately compels you
to laugh at the man behind his back ; and (b) when

(a)

the man is quite poor : this is not so funny but, of
course, means that you can laugh in his face, if you can
bear the proximity.

The other joke, as everyone knows, is Buying The
Horse.

This is the joke-royal among Horsemen and loses nothing by being so eminently *practical*. The point is that *one of you is always 'done'* (Hurrah!). Get this clear: buying and selling horses isn't Trade or anything sordid like that; it is a joke. Hurrah for the friend who 'did' you, he was so clever, and you are a

sportsman. Hurrah for you if you 'did' him, particularly if you cheated: it is his turn now to be a sportsman (Yoiks! Hoots! Got-away-with-it!).

But don't let your sense of humour run away with you. All this applies to horses only. If after a few successful deals in horse-flesh you try a similar deal at, say, Contract Bridge you will be hounded out of the Portland Club.

But you have not yet purchased your first animal. It is time you were up and doing, being done, etc. So think of an uncle, double round to him, show him your poverty-mark and borrow one hundred pounds off him (on the ground that you are almost a g*ntl*m*n and would like to make a finished job of it). Then let it be known quietly in sporting circles that you are in the market for a ' handy-English-Hunter-with-no-dam-circus-tricks-about-it '. A few seconds after doing this, you will receive one hundred sacrificial offers of splendid horses which, having apparently no uncles, are going begging. But beware ! To avoid making a per-manently discouraging purchase read :

CHAPTER II

HORSES TO AVOID

THERE is an old saying, ' No foot, no horse ' ; so you will naturally refuse to buy any horse which has not the full set of (four) feet.

You will also avoid 'U-Necked' or 'V-Necked'
Horses (very discouraging) and those dangerous 'wall-

eyed' animals (which go about looking for walls to
dash into or smash your legs against), and, above all,
the rare but permanently discouraging stamp of horse
known as a 'Strawberry Roach'.

You will remember also that a good horse, though it
need not be a thorough-bred, must be 'sound' in the
legs, or steady on its thorough-pins as horsemen
say, and also 'sound in wind', by which horsemen

mean that its breathing should make no noticeable sound at all, as a horse which ' whistles ' is rather irritating, particularly if, as so often is the case, it *always whistles the same tune.*

Then, of course, there are the questions of *Age* and *Lameness.* Everyone knows what a bore it is trying to help lame dogs over stiles ; heaving lame horses over five-barred gates is, as any hunting-man will agree, a *positively crashing bore.*

You should therefore avoid purchasing any horses which are warranted to be permanently lame, in spite of what Capt. Pontoon[1] (*Dirigible Quadrupeds,* p. 109) says about horses which are permanently lame on three legs being curable by deliberately laming the fourth leg, ' *thus rendering them, in effect, sound* '

[1] Capt. W. D. Pontoon, M.C., B.S.A., R.E., author of *Dirigible Quadrupeds,* etc.

Capt. P., as everyone knows, is himself by no means a sound authority.

Finally, the question of Age. Everyone knows that the way to tell if a horse is too young or too old is to look at its teeth, and that the older the horse the longer the teeth and, of course, vice versa.

TOO YOUNG   TOO OLD

CHAPTER III

VICE (OOH !)

But the most important thing in a horse is its manners. In rejecting any but a well-behaved beast you will have the support of all the old stable-sayings—' Horses, like men, are best judged by their actions ', ' Kind hearts are more than coronets ', ' Handsome is as handsome cab ', etc. etc.

Above all, you will avoid horses addicted to Vice. Fortunately, since the Hunters Improvement Society took matters in hand horses' manners have improved enormously, but there are still many animals about

Scraping aside the bedding.

with *most objectionable habits ;* and the frightful thing is that many of these vices are *catching.* Consequently, if you do not buy with great caution you may find that after associating for some weeks with your horse you have become incurably addicted to, say, *scraping aside the bedding* (your wife will be furious), or *eating it* (divorce inevitable) ; *tearing the clothes or bandages with the teeth* (awkward if you ever go into hospital) ; *cow-kicking* (for which you will be viciously prosecuted by the R.S.P.C.A.), *crib-biting* ('ware R.S.P.C.C.), or even ' biting the groom or attendant while being

rubbed down ', which causes endless trouble in a Turkish Bath.

* * *

Very well, then : we have warned you against the worst ; but do not lose heart and go weakly to some reputable Horse Dealer who is such a rotten sportsman he won't even try to sell horses unless they are warranted sound in every way by some reputable Horse Surgeon. Play the game ; buy your experience like a man—remember that the only occasion on which

the great ' Nimrod ' owns to having been thoroughly
had about the Horse was when he bought (in the year
1818) ' a very clever well-bred young horse the property
of a clergyman in Bedfordshire '—and buy boldly from
your friends and relations even if some of these turn
out to be very clever well-bred old clergymen in
Bedfordshire.

BIT IV
RIDING IT

POINTS OF THE HORSEMAN

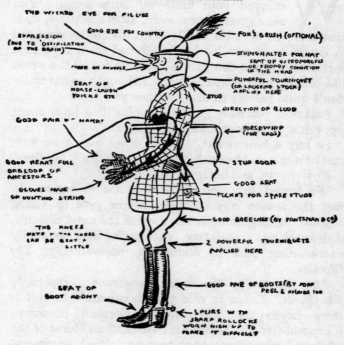

THE WICKED EYE FOR FILLIES

GOOD EYE FOR COUNTRY

EXPRESSION (DUE TO OSSIFICATION OF THE BRAIN)

NOSE OR SNUFFLE

SEAT OF HORSE-LAUGH YOICKS ETC

GOOD PAIR OF HANDS

GOOD HEART FULL OF BLOOD OF ANCESTORS

GLOVES MADE OF HUNTING STRING

THE KNEES NOTE: THE KNEES CAN BE BENT A LITTLE

SEAT OF BOOT ONLY

FOX'S BRUSH (OPTIONAL)

STRING HALTER FOR HAT SEAT OF OSTEOPOROSIS OR PRONGY CONDITION OF THE HEAD

POWERFUL TOURNIQUET (OR LAUGHING STOCK) APPLIED HERE

STUD

DIRECTION OF BLOOD

HORSEWHIP (FOR CADS)

STUD BOOK

GOOD SEAT

POCKET FOR SPARE STUDS

GOOD BREECHES (BY PANTIMAN & CO)

2 POWERFUL TOURNIQUETS APPLIED HERE

GOOD PAIR OF BOOTS (BY JOHN PEEL & HOUNDS TOO)

SPURS WITH SHARP ROLLOCKS WORN HIGH UP TO MAKE IT DIFFICULT

29

CHAPTER I

100% OF THE DANGER

> ' " Mary, Mary, veterinary,
> How does your bedroom go ? "
> " With swingle-trees,
> And saddle-trees,
> And boot-trees all in a row." '

WELL, you have *bought it* (dammit), and enjoyed your first real horse-laugh. You were green ; you were, asyermightsay, dun. But there he is in his stable, with his ankles wrapped in cotton-wool and his head tethered by a rope to a sort of sliding wooden turnip—looking for all the world like other people's bay spaldings, although you naturally don't quite believe in his existence yet. . . .

And now you have got to ride him (bad luck, cheer up, gee up, etc., especially the horse).

So buy a bowler hat, cram it down over your ears and halter it to the back of your neck with a bootlace.

Now do you feel better ? Not much ?

We feared so : and there is worse to come. In fact the reason why so many people give up riding right at the beginning is this : quite the most difficult, disheartening, dislocating, excoriating and generally excruciating part of Riding is, undoubtedly, *The Clothes.*

Also by 100% the most dangerous ; especially *The Boots.* Learn to ride your boots and the rest is mere horse-play ! A famous German horseman (Corporal-General Baron Fixt von und zu Horst of the 18/70th Umlauts) is said to have exclaimed, on observ-

ing some British Cavalry Officers at Mons, " *Aller
Bompfen !* Men who can defeat such boots are
ungekriegsbomstrafendlich ".

But the Cavalry are not so invincible as von Horst
believed. Everyone knows that officers of ' The

Do you feel better ?

Bays'' *never dance ;* but not many people *know why.*
It is quite simple ; they have never been able to get
their boots off in time. Indeed most of the senior
officers in our Mounted Regiments are still wearing to
this day the polo-boots in which they first paraded as
Subalterns—not for reasons of economy, or from mere
conservatism either ; the truth is, they have not yet
succeeded in getting out of those boots—they are,
asyermightsay, literally hide-bound.

And it is a frightful fact that even for our English hunting-women with their perfect riding legs there is only one thing more dangerous, more hopelessly dreadful than getting into riding-boots, and that is—getting out of them again. It is fruitless, or, worse still, bootless to deny it.

But you, Sir, must never give in, even if your insteps do. All the greatest authorities from Geoffrey Gambado to Sir Walter Gilbey are agreed that it is a rider's duty to dress as uncomfortably as possible. For which reason they have laid down that The Garments should be only less dangerous and disheartening than The Boots, and should consist, in essence, of powerful *tourniquets*, applied at the knees and neck, designed to drive the blood away from the feet and head (where the Horseman will never miss it) and concentrate it at the parts he thinks with, namely his hands and his seat. (Examine minutely Disheartening Diagram on p. 29.)

Nobody is more particular about all this than the Horse itself. One of the first things a horse does is to look at your boots and breeches. And if the former are too short or the latter have the buttons on the

Incorrect

outside of the knees, then Woa betide you—the Horse will not go.

Thoroughbreds will not allow a man even to mount them unless his breeches are cut by Tyghtz or Pantsman or one of the very few other tailors who are recognised by the Best Horses.

And it is entirely due to their carelessness about *kit* that Cowboys, Australians, Canadian North-West Mounted Police, Mexicans and other obstinate natives ride in such an amateurish and incorrect style.

Mexicans, for instance, insist on riding in leather beach-pyjamas, while cowboys clothe their legs in hearth-rugs and the North-West 'Mounties' in long laced skating-boots!

You, however, will never descend to such rotten form (especially in Rotten Row) but devote your

To inspect their studs

attention to the great object of making yourself look (except when hunting) as much like a jockey's apprentice as possible.

So, to begin with, take a pair of binoculars and some notebooks and go up on the Downs and *study form.* Note every strap and button worn by the stable-boys, stud-grooms and other leaders of fashion. One of the most striking proofs of the importance attached by horsemen to Clothes is the way the Best People regularly call round at their friends' stables merely to *inspect their Studs.* Keep a special notebook for these last, a big one with STUD-BOOK printed on it in gold

letters ; and read all the textbooks you can find on
the subject of riding-kit (except the one by Capt.
Pontoon entitled *With Moss Bros. at Ascot*, as this is,
we are informed, a dud-book).

CHAPTER II

GETTING ON

> ' Prepare to Mount.'
> Old Cavalry Threat.

THREE years elapse : and you have mastered your kit.
Even the boots (or your feet) are so well broken-in
that you are no longer forced to go to bed in your
spurs. You have suffered. Deep lines of suffering are
visible around your mouth, your neck, and particularly
round about the back of your knees. Life holds very
little meaning for you. You are almost a Horseman...

Compared with what you have been through in the
way of agony, money, etc., in order to get your Clothes
right, Riding will be a bagatelle, a mere game of pitch
and toss.

So lead out the iron-grey spalding (it will be about
middle-aged by now) and prepare to *mount*.

*   *   *

According to all the most manly authorities the idea
is now to *spring lightly into the saddle*. This is, however,
easier to write than to do : so persuade the spalding
to *lie down as for sleep*, or even actually lull it to
slumber ; grip it between the knees (your own, of
course) ; then, strike it sharply with the spurs, *thus*

Figs. V–VIII

causing it to spring lightly on to its feet. Alternatively, follow the directions in Figs. V–VIII.

But, before doing this, estimate carefully the *width* of your mount, since nothing is so irritating as to find you have 'overreached', or surmounted the beast entirely, and, having landed on the further side, are now technically 'off-side'.

*   *   *

Well, you are 'up'.

But are you the right way up?

Shade the eyes and gaze searchingly in front of you. What is the outlook? A lot of horse-hair. No doubt, but does the hair climb steeply upwards, culminating in the pointed ears mentioned in Bit II, Chapter I? Or does the hair tail off declivitously towards the ground? If the latter, you have commenced mounting by *placing the wrong foot in the stirrup* and are now definitely the wrong way 'up'.

Continue mounting until you envisage the ears quite clearly in front of you. But look for them closely, because the ears can be folded back by the horse so as to become invisible to any but a trained

CORRECT OUTLOOK   INCORRECT

observer. If in doubt, *shout* ('Whelps !', 'Hackaway !', etc.)—the ears will then rise to the occasion and possibly the whole horse, too, so be ready to hold on with tooth and nail, might and (of course) mane, boot and saddle, and so on (for the moment).

CHAPTER III

A GOOD PAIR OF HANDS

> ' It never reins but it paws.'
> Old Riding School Saying.

' ONCE up, three things only are necessary : *A Good Seat, A Good Pair of Hands,* and *Plenty of Pluck* ' (Col: Numnah-Smith).

NOTE :—According to Capt. Pontoon, on the other hand, what the beginner needs most is ' a hard head, soft ground for it to strike, and plenty of luck (*Dirigible Quadrupeds*, Chap. III).[1]

Take the hands first ; there must be two (2) ; with fingers (not all thumbs), and they should instinctively take up the reins in a symmetrical and horsemanlike manner. If they do not they are not a good pair of hands, in fact probably not even a pair (and you yourself are not a born horseman after all but probably of foreign extraction).

Moreover, if you find on close examination that there are no deep slots between the fingers (these slots are designed by Providence to receive the reins) you are, once again, not a born rider but a born Channel-swimmer (Webb-fingered, asyermightsay) and will always have to ride with a single rein.

CONTROVERSIAL SEATS

Left: forward seat, recommmended for stumblers.
Centre: backward seat, recommended for rearers.
Right: wrong, not recommended at all.

So much for the hands: as to The Seat, little, obviously, can be said with propriety ; except that after your first few rides you will definitely have a *bad seat*—it is galling, but inevitable—but that as time,

[1] In our endeavour to be scrupulously fair, i.e. neither partial nor impartial, we feel bound to quote not only from the best but also from the worst possible authorities.

embrocation, etc., goes on, your Seat will get better
and better until you enjoy the supreme honour, which
only equestrians achieve, of having it openly praised
by strangers.

CHAPTER IV

THE HORSE IN MOTION

*' The Horse is a natural jumper, and if properly
handled by an experienced rider possessed of a
good pair of hands, breeches, and boots, will never
refuse timber, water, rasper or oxer.'*
COL. NUMNAH-SMITH.

*' The horse is an unreliable bounder and will refuse
anything except oats.'* CAPT. PONTOON.

IN its anxiety to amuse the Best People, bemuse
the Proletariat and generally make a lot of names for
itself, the Horse has developed a number of peculiar
' gaits ', ' paces ' or methods of prancing, lolloping,
lumbering, gadding and galumphing about.   For
instance, all horses can jog, jib, jog-trot, jib-trot, walk
(except when required), cantle, stumble and stop
(especially when tired).   Most horses can gallop
(usually in one directly only—see Bit V, Stables,
Feeding, etc.) and exceptional breeds can also cavort
or caracol, amble or tripple, jink, jiggle and (except
when required) jump.

Of these disturbing movements we shall describe
only one, The Jump, which is the rarest but also the
best for talking about after dinner as the Port wine
goes decantering by.

According to Cropper, the famous scientific authority

on equitation, the Jump is usually executed by the Horse in one or more of the following ways :

'A. On approaching the obstacle too slowly the front legs are suddenly elevated and replaced with great force together with the rest of the horse, on or in the obstacle according as the latter be convex or concave. B. On approaching too near the obstacle the front legs are suddenly elevated, thus striking the obstacle (if convex) with great force ; the rest of the horse then describes an arc pivoting upon the point of impact and returns to earth on the further side of the obstacle stomach upwards. The rider on the other hand is never able to describe anything in connection with the affair, having been thrown suddenly forward on to his head (which is now concave). C. On approaching the slightest obstacle the front legs are suddenly propped on to the ground, the centre of depravity of the brute being simultaneously thrown *backwards* on to the haunches, and the rider *forwards* on to the horse's head. (This is the position known as The Forward Seat.)'

A

The third method so clearly described by Cropper

is undoubtedly the most usual of the three ways of jumping favoured by the horse ; but it should be noted that retired horsemen, and others whose views are particularly severe, maintain that this method is never instigated by the horse at all but is the result of a failure to instigate (or psychological Moment of Inertia) on the part of the rider.

NOTE :—If you are determined to talk like a regular steeplejack about the big jumps, you might try going to a riding-school where you will learn to jump by numnahs, i.e. you will practise doing it without reins or stirrups or saddle or enthusiasm, and pretty often without the horse either.

CHAPTER V

YOU'RE OFF !

JUMPING aside, there is no need for you to attempt to dictate to The Horse at first which of its various ' paces ' it should adopt : the first thing is to get started. So gather up all the reins you can see into an orderly bundle (using the slots between the fingers whenever possible), straighten your tie, tighten your lips, girths, hat-band, etc., rub the sharp rullocks of your spurs up and down the horse's sides—and you're off !

Get on again, therefore ; in spite of any impressions you may have to the contrary, you are not yet a *finished horseman.* (See finished picture overleaf.)

Finished horseman

CHAPTER VI

FIRST AIDS AND SECOND AIDS

'Come hup! I say, you hugly beast!'
MR. JORROCKS.

LONG before you are properly on again you will find
that the Horse is jogging off vaguely in some direction
or other dictated by the Horse's marvellous sense of
some direction or other. Let it. Anything is better
at this stage than an altercation with the horse ; and
nothing could be worse than going through the antics
depicted in Figs. V–VIII again. Never mind what
sort of fig. you cut this time, but scramble into the
saddle by any means, however squalid, and remember
that *' the horse is always right.'*[1]

Nevertheless, the rider is permitted to help the
horse by certain means called ' The Aids '. There

[1] Col: N.-S., and all retired horsemen, are agreed on this point.

are two kinds of Aids : *First Aids*—consisting of
the ' Gee-up ' for starting the horse, the ' Woa ' for
stopping it, and the ' *** ! ' for remonstrating with the
*** ; and *Second Aids*—consisting of various pressures
of the bit, reins and leg on the lips, reins and other
suitable bits of the horse.

For instance, if you apply the *left rein* and the *right
leg*, that is supposed to help the horse turn to the *left*,
and vice versa : and if you apply the right rein and
the right leg to the (right) horse, the animal should
walk sideways (to the left) or ' passage ', as it is called
(since if you had to ride down a passage it would be
obviously more daring to do it broadside on).

Very well then ; it is obvious that you should now
apply all these various Aids, remedies, stimulants and
narcotics in turn (*not* all at once) and observe the
effect on your horse, your seat, your clothes, etc., and
note it down in your Stud Book ; but never forget
that, whatever happens, *the horse is always right*. For
instance, if the horse on feeling a firm pressure of the
left rein and wrong leg runs rapidly to the nearest
tree and attempts to scrape you off against it—the
horse is quite right. Most probably your breeches are
badly cut or made of inferior cloth.

*   *   *

There is one other Aid which we have hesitated to
mention because it is *so frightfully cruel ;* and that is,
throat-lashing. No textbook will definitely recommend
the throat-lash as an Aid ; and yet—well, there it is
. . . (ask any horseman).

While on this painful subject we should, perhaps,
advise you that the Horsewhip is never used for

lashing the Horse. It is only used (by Horsemen, of course) for thrashing fellows who do not ride to hounds —in fact cads of any kind—*within an inch of their lives.* The etiquette is very strong on this point ; so, as you will be pretty sure (later on when you are a real Horseman) to have to deal with a cad now and then, you had better get one of those horsewhips (see Fig. IX) which are conveniently marked out in inches.

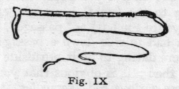

Fig. IX

In the end, of course, you will learn to judge the thing at a glance. . . .

Judge the *thing* at a glance

CHAPTER VII

RIDE STRAIGHT

> ' Give me *another* Horse—
> bind up my wounds.'
> RICH. III.

BUT we are losing your grip. You are, we trust, still
' up '. Your task for the present is to learn to RIDE
STRAIGHT—do not be confused by the fact that some
women ride at right angles as a matter of Habit—but
square up to it, instigate your Dumb Friend by
hollowing the tongue and ejaculating a loud ' nick-
nick ', or punching its flanks indefatigably with your
heels (unless, of course, you are still wearing those
spurs), or by cracking your horsewhip as far away
from your face as possible, or something.

Well done ! The animal's feet splash out in all
directions ; it breathes outwards continuously in a
menacing fashion ; its head, becoming suddenly quite
loose and much nearer to you than ever before, points
up and down and even right and left in a most untrustworthy manner. Splendid ! You are undoubtedly
Riding, or something. But are you *riding straight ?*
Look at your horse's *whithers* (if you have forgotten
where they are, look at page 10 again) : disregard
the head, it is untrustworthy ; only by regarding the
whithers can you tell what direction you are going in.
And disregard that loud clink-clinking noise down
below—it is nothing, just a spot of pastern slap. . . .

Now feel your horse's mouth. It feels like lead ?
Try a firmer pressure. Try pulling the reins like mad.

The horse is pulling like mad, too ? The pace grows hotter ? The horse is running away with you ! Never mind ; you are riding straight ; straight for a haystack or straight for a chalk-quarry, it doesn't matter. . . .

Look out now ! Hold hard ! Thump ! We knew it : Your iron-grey spalding has lost control of its thoroughpins, floundered, *and done the splints*. . . .

Done ' The Splints '

* * *

Well, call it a day. Sing it a Pollywollydoodle : nominate it anything you like ; you have *plenty to talk about* now. You have ridden straight, you have headed for Crumpleton Quarry, your horse has done a terrifically technical thing, you've taken your first toss, you have been bumped off and are still alive !

So reassemble your disjointed steed and lead it quietly back to the stable. It is swelling a little, maybe, at various points, but that is no matter of yours; you yourself are swelling all over with pride and precipices and the knowledge that having done ten minutes' solo equitation on the horse you are now entitled to do about ten hours' solo expatiation on it (a fair ratio), and are in fact *practically a horseman.*

Go home then, and practise the True Art: assemble your household and tell them *how the brute fought for his head, how you groped for his tail, how hot the pace was* and *how red your face was,* how the lower you rode down in the saddle the higher your shirt rode up round your middle, how splendidly your boots behaved and how you finally *came a crupper and nearly broke your neck* (Whoopee!).

Then tell them all over again in even more quadrupedantic language. And if any of them look bored, or try to sneak away—*throat-lash'em! It is your birthright and your right. . . .*

BIT V

THE HORSE AT HOME

CHAPTER I

STABLE TALK

' Make much of your horse : no one else will.'
CAPT. W. D. PONTOON.

WELL, you have got the whip-hand now ;
but mere equestrianism is not enough, you
are not yet a True and Complete Horseman,
you have still a lot to learn . . . manners, for instance.

Foreigners and other second-best people are often
over-anxious about their table-manners. The Best
People take such trifles, truffles, asparagi, etc., in their
stride and concentrate on Stable-manners. They are
right ; because, as Col: Numnah-Smith insists, ' the
Quality of the Horse's Owner is always Apparent from
the Appearance of the Owner's Horse '.

So refrain from *smoking cigars* in the Stable (nothing
burns faster, once it gets the butt between its teeth,
than a horse-on-fire) ; *lift your feet* on quitting the
stall, so as not to disturb the litter (there are always
too many puppies round stables, anyway—see also,
later, Dogs in Manger, etc., p. 59) ; and remember to
chew bits of straw incessantly ; or your horses will give
your lack of Quality away by Appearing Permanently

Sick with Shame when Col: N.-S. or any other expert horseman drops in to inspect you and your stables.

And, above all, do try not to lock the stable door after the horse has been stolen : it was a fashionable practice at one time, no doubt, but Crocker and Geoffrey Gambado, and Geoffrey Brooke, and Geoffrey Crascredo, and all the best authorities on horse-management are dead against it. Just leave the stable door half open—the thief might repent and bring the horse back (especially if it was rather moth-ridden), or some herds of wild horses might trot in and you could use them for dragging things out of people, or something. . . . On the other hand, don't lock the door *before* the horse has been stolen—you may lose the key, or go away for the week-end and forget about the horse and by the time you come back it will have gone bad or something. . . .

Finally, your stable-manners will never be perfect unless you do everything correctly *according to Crocker*. So do try to find someone who knows who Crocker was, especially if there is anybody.

Similarly, among the best people, Table Talk and Stable Talk are one and the same thing. Once you decide to take up your birthright and become a True Horseman you are let off for life talking at dinner about Politics, or Books (except 'Jorrocks') or anything except hay-boxes and stringhalters and the innumerable Chronic, Cholic and Comic Ailments which Horses contract, swell up into and burst of.

But before attempting advanced stable-talk of this nature it is usual, unusual, etc., to master the straight-forward patter which concerns grooming the horse, watering the animal, feeding the brute, shoeing the quadruped, summering the beast (in summer) and unsummering the hairy nuisance again in time for the hunting-season.

To begin, then, with the stable itself. ' The Stable ', as all absolute experts insist, ' should be not too small ; and at the same time not too large '. Absolutely : if too small, you may find it impossible to insert the horse absolutely into the stable ; while if too large it causes a great waste of straw, etc., under which the horse might get lost, or hide, for absolutely days on end. (See overleaf.)

The same is true of the bed-stall, or head-sitting-room, for single horse ; and in this connection it is useful, useless, etc., to remember that ' a horse when extended at full gallop covers two furloughs in a minute, but when lying down at full length considerably less—though it can, of course, keep this up all night if not disturbed '.[1]

The Stable . . . should be not too small . . .

The stall should therefore be considerably less than 2 furloughs in length and should contain plenty of bedding (horse-blankets, horse-bolsters and horse-water bottles), since every considerate Owner likes to see all his animals thoroughly tucked-up when they come home after exercise ; though, as a matter of fact, all horses *can sleep standing up* (like Policemen). Again, straw should be liberally provided, as horses

[1] Capt. Pontoon, *Dirig: Quad:*, p. 207.

like to while away the time by plaiting it into their tails and manes.

. . . a great waste of straw, under which the horse
might get lost, or hide, for days . . .

CHAPTER II

HOW TO DRESS A HORSE

> ' In time of War the use of curry-combs to remove mud is forbidden.'
>
> Art. XLVIII, Haig Convention.

> ' Give a horse a bad mane, and bang it ! '
>
> Old Stable Saying.

IF you overhear a Superhorseman saying something about *dressing* a horse, do not run away with the idea that he is referring to those elegant little eighteenth-century straw hats, with holes for the ears to poke out of, with which Good Farmers crown their cart-horses in summer ; or even to those romantic hooded cloaks, with holes for the eyes to look out of, which are used to disguise race-horses as bogies (see dressy pictures above).

' Dressing ' horses merely means scraping the dirt off them and then sharpening and stropping and polishing all the various Points of the Horse, and there is nothing romantic about it except that it is also called

' grooming ' after Lord Grougham who invented the art.

In grooming, no labour-saving devices are allowed—the idea being to make grooming, like riding, as difficult as possible—and the only authorised tools are the *body-brush* with which it is very difficult to get the mud, scurf, etc., out of the horse's fur ; the *curry-comb*, with which it is almost impossible to get the mud, scurf, etc., out of the body-brush ; the *dandy-brush*, which is comparatively useful and therefore comparatively discouraged ; and the wisp, a complicated straw sausage made with great difficulty and used for drying damp horses (damping dry horses, etc.) because straw is so absorbent.

To groom the horse, place a straw in the mouth and make a low, continuous hissing sound through the straw—otherwise proceed as for beating a suit or cleansing a carpet. Be careful to put the straw into your own mouth, not the Horse's, because (*a*) the horse cannot be relied on not to swallow the straw and (*b*) cannot be relied on to make the hissing sound.

* * *

Besides this everyday horsemaid's work there is a certain amount of beauty-treatment to be done, such as clipping the heels, pruning the ears, singeing the beard, and filing (and marking) the teeth, before a horse is really ready for show.

The treatment of the tail is also of great importance (especially in times of war). There is only one correct way of grooming the tail : the hair must be ' pulled ' from underneath (see Art. XLVI, Haig Convention).[1]

[1] Failure to observe this rule was responsible for some of the worst artillery disasters in the late war.

To pull a horse's tail, stand well to one side and make soothing cries such as 'gid-over-yold-buzzard!'. Otherwise proceed as for plucking a fowl or wife's eyebrows.

The tail may also be 'banged' (provided the horse is good-natured), or it can be dry-docked, i.e. bitten off short in early youth. Squeamish people say it is cruel to dock a horse of its tail ; others who are fond of insects and do not mind the taste of horsehair say it is cruel to the horse-flies *not* to remove the Horse's tail. And in any case it would be cruel to sporting American visitors to abandon docking, as the sight of an English horse with a docked tail never fails to amuse them.

*   *   *

Lastly we come to the controversial question— should the horse be washed ? Very few people know the right answer, but as a matter of fact it is—Yes : there is no truth in the panicky rumour that horses are liable to *shrink* in the wash (except, of course, the

special breed of shetland-wool ponies, which have already shrunk enough and if washed any more would probably become first woolly sheep and then woolly caterpillars and finally minute particles of fluff invisible to the naked eye).

CHAPTER III

FEEDING THE BRUTE

' *You can lead a horse to water, but you can't make it think.*'　　　CAPT. PONTOON.[1]

NORWEGIAN horses will eat *fish*, and Indian horses *moth*, but on the whole horses are more particular about what they eat than about what they drink— though they will not drink capped hock, calked champagne or greasy heel-taps of any kind. Horses, however, are fond of beer and whisky ; but you must not give your brute too much of these or it may turn into a regular horse-toper, or, as horsemen say, ' go groggy '. A horse that is always drunk is a bad horse, and nothing is more distressing to sober-minded people than to see a horse (or a g*ntl*m*n) in that condition, ambling about bumping and boring everybody. . . .

All horses are addicted to the low-bred or cock-tail habit of drinking just before meals, though it is only fair to say that since the introduction of the tee-totalisator race-horses at least drink practically nothing but water.

But it is difficult to blame the horse for any of this,

[1] Capt. Pontoon is wrong as usual : the truth is, you can lead a horse to water, but you can't *make it sink*.

Bumping and boring everybody. . . .

since it is condemned to eat such uninteresting meals,
i.e. handfuls of dry oats, the tops of dry stable doors,
etc.—the nearest thing to a succulent *entremet* it ever

sees being a beautiful brown jelly made of linseed
which, as every cavalry recruit knows, looks much
more savoury than it tastes.

*   *   *

A word of warning : when out riding do not allow
your horse to snatch at every sprig of green it passes—
or one day it will eat Yew, which is fatal for it.
Similarly, in stables, do not allow it to snatch at every

stable-boy that passes or indulge it in any way with
human flesh—or one day it will *eat You.* . . .

And another rule of the ' *Oat École* ' is never to give

a horse bread. There is a dreadful (in fact breadful) malady called ' Bread-in-the-bone '. . . .

* * *

And one word more : as well as a hay-rack there is a *Manger* in all the best stalls and loose-boxes. *Dogs* should therefore never be allowed in the stable, for obvious reasons. . . .

CHAPTER IV

UNDER THE SPREADING HORSE-NUT CHEST

' Couldn't say " Shoe ! " to a Blacksmith.'
Old Sporting Taunt.

EVERYONE knows that horses wear iron horseshoes (for luck) on their feet or *joghpaws* (as they are called in India) ; and that the shoes wear out in time and have to be replaced by the village Blacksmith (or *Harrier*, as he is often called because of his hairy arms, brawny beard and general nappiness).

In former days, before the difference between the fore feet and the hind feet was clearly understood, the Blacksmith used to begin by spreading his chest under a standing horse-nut tree and *pairing the feet* (two fore, two hind, two near, two off; total 4, not 8, as some of them are duplicates); but that is all out-of-date; nowadays, after a brief manicure with the largest size nail-file imaginable, one gets on with the fixing of the shoe by hammering nails into the horse's foot.

But do not allow yourself to be carried away by the discovery that the horse is almost the only animal that you can hammer nails into with success; don't try to hammer nails into it in all sorts of places—in order to fix the saddle firmly on the back, for instance, or even to prevent the nose-bag continually coming off. That would be unsuccessful.

Nor should you make the mistake of thinking that the hoof itself is just a solid lump of animal cork. On the contrary, it is full of Coronets, Cushions, Coffins, Leaves and, amazing as it may seem, there are *Frogs in it* (ask any horseman). These frogs go in pairs ; a Sensitive Frog and an Insensitive Frog. The latter, of course, can look after itself, but all good-hearted riders take the greatest care not to hurt the feelings of the Sensitive Frog in the slightest degree. (See heart-rending song about this in Bit VIII, *The Horse In Literature*.)

NOTE :—Horses are far too intelligent not to want to kick each other sometimes ; it is advisable therefore when potting horses out to grass (' summering ') to remove the hind shoes. And since horses are apt to make themselves ill by rushing about in the sun and then plunging into ponds, it might be a good idea to unscrew the hind legs as well—horse-surgeons will do almost anything, as well as almost nothing, for three guineas.

CHAPTER V

DREADFUL DISEASES OF THE HORSE

' They say, Old Man, that your horse is dead,
And we say so
And we hope so.'   Sea-chanty.

' O Dear, what can the Matter be.'
Old Vegetinary Dirge.

THE horse enjoys ill-health in so many thousands of ways that only a brief selection of the most dreadful can be given, but these should prove sufficient to enable you to talk learnedly about the noble animal

- - -

for, say, ten years ; by which time you will no doubt
have been able to invent an equal number of special
varieties founded on your own experience, errors, etc.

Some diseases of the horse are, as we have indicated,
not *catching*, but others, such as the Common Cranial
disease known as Osteoporosis (swollen or spongy
condition of the head), are definitely contagious.
Horsemen should guard against this disease by means
of ambitious marriages, highbrows, Australians, etc.

THE VEG:

All horses being vegetarians, it is only right that
when your horse is ill you should have to send for the
special kind of doctor called a Vegetinary Surgeon, or,
more vulgarly, ' The Veg:',[1] who specialises in horses.

The Veg: is the most remarkable kind of doctor in
existence because, although a genuine surgeon, he
never operates, and because he is *always right ;* he is
able to diagnose a Colic, infallibly, every time.

This is how it is done. One day when you visit
your horse it appears ill : it is obviously in pain. You
are afraid it may have got tired of your lemon-yellow
waistcoat or have taken a dislike to the cut of your
leggings. You go away and change all your clothes ;
but the horse is still poorly. You try everything, your
jodhpores, your Newmarket boots ; you put on all
your polo things, including the great big artificial
knee-caps which polomen wear to make their legs look
like horse's legs. No good. Finally you put on full
hunting-kit and blow ' Come to the Cookhouse Door '
several times with your hunting-horn. The horse pays

---

[1] Cf. the well-known stable picture by Alken entitled ' A Joint
and Two Veg:.'

no need. It does not even respond by blowing ' The
Last Post Toastie ' with its nostrils.

Then you know it is time to send for the Veg:
because the horse is definitely ill inside. The Veg:
comes and you ask him what is wrong ; he examines
the animal's eyes, nostrils, mouth, etc., and says the
horse has a bad Colic.

The next time your horse is ill the same thing
happens. In fact whenever your horse is ill inside the
same thing will always happen. At first you will be
surprised that whenever your horse is ill inside it
always has the same disease. But in time you will
learn (though no horseman will tell you) that a Colic
is the only inside illness a horse can have. And if by
any chance you become a priest, one day a Vegetinary
Surgeon will confess to you (among other things) that
the word Colic means, simply, *an illness inside a
horse.* . . .

The Veg: is therefore always right in his diagnosis ;
which gives him and the horse-owner great confidence.

You cannot, of course, give the horse confidence,
too ; all you can do is to give it a huge pill or ' horse-
ball ' (or *mare nostrum*) made of—

Oil of Sandstone	10 drachms
Carbolic Soapsuds	10 quackms
Bitter Aloes	2 bits
Lot of Enoes	2 lots
Essence of Nazipan	2 pnsfl
Spirit of Bombazine	2 much
Sweet gunpowder	a whiff
Gall & Wormwood	quad: stuff:

(Add Cardamoms, Poppadums, Turpentine, and

Patum Pepperiums, and roll into a ball with Molasses, Linseed and Legerdemain.)

The ' ball ' is pushed down the horse's throat by hand, or blown down it by means of a large tube held between your teeth.

NOTE :—When using the tube method remember that the horse can blow too ; it is therefore up to you to *blow first.* . . .

If the mixture will not stay rolled up in a ball it can be given in liquid form ; instead of ' balling ' the horse you ' drench ' it, i.e. just mix the medicine in a hunting-horn and pour it on the horse's head, but *not* down its ear as that leads nowhere.

Lameness (or laminitis as horsemen often call it) may be due to disease, injury, or pure straightforward shamming ; and is rendered more interesting by the fact that your horse may limp, either periodically or permanently, on any of its two fore, two hind, two near, all four, or too far off, legs ; and also at any one, two, three or more of its numerous paces, or even when lying down in the stable.

Excessive lameness is sometimes caused by the joint
being actually dislocated (due to excessively disjointed
horsemanship) ; fortunately many Hunts now employ
the services of a Joint-Master who should be sent for
immediately in extreme cases.

*   *   *

WINDGALL, BOG-SPAVIN, FARCY, THRUSH, HUMOUR, SWINGLES, FLANDERS, BLINKERS, SYMBIOTIC MANGE, AND THAT WILL DO FOR THE PRESENT

All the above are genuine mentionable Diseases of
the Horse and the following facts about them were
confided to the Authors by *Dr. Green* himself, the
oldest and most illustrious of horse-doctors.

Irish hunters are particularly liable to *Bog-spavins*,
which are the result of sitting too long in damp bogs

(Cure: drain the bogs); but handy-English-hunters are even more liable to *Dog*-spavins, which result from sitting about too long on hounds (Cure: train the dogs).

Other miseries worth mentioning are, *Wind-galls*, which are cured by ointment (and not, as you might easily imagine, bicarbonate of soda); and *Matter in the Foot* (send for the Veg: and ask what *is* the matter); and *Swingles* (caused by the horse rashly eating of the fruit of the Swingle-Tree); and *Sand-Colic* (caused by having wars in deserts); and *Hand-Colic* (caused by Lack of Legerdemain when administering horse-balls); *Flanders*, a depressive neurosis affecting both horse and man (due to sitting in septic mud for years on end— cure, keep end as dry as possible); and beyond all, the *Epizoötic Sniggers or T. Webster's Disease.*

The Epizoötic Sniggers

*   *   *

Humour in the horse is a form of disease and invariably futile ; it takes two forms. The most common is, *small lumps under the skin* (Lumpas)—which the horse produces quietly after eating too many beans or peas or indian corns, the joke being when the inexperienced horseman thinks the lumps are actually the beans or peas—whereas the horse knows perfectly well that they are just lumps.

The more serious form of humorous disorder, or Frolic, is when the horse attempts to turn the whole thing—grooming, feeding, hunting, everything—into a farce (by playing the foal, etc.). This is the condition known as *Farcy*, and when, as sometimes happens, the rider becomes infected too the consequences are very, very distressing. (See v. distressing picture below.)

'Farcy'

With horses as with humans, stamping the feet, rubbing the legs and kicking at inoffensive objects are a sign of some form of Irritation, often due in the case of horses to *Symbiotic Mange*, but in humans not frightfully often.

Another sign to watch for is *Staring*.   If your horse

only stares at you with its eyes it is probably just wondering about your breeches or boots and if these are satisfactory no harm need be anticipated.   But if it starts staring harshly at you *with its coat*, the horse is diseased ; send for the Veg: at once, and whatever you do *don't stare back*, especially with your coat.

But the most dreadful of all the Diseases of the Horse is undoubtedly The Thrush. Think of it !

When the horse gets the Thrush it becomes subject to an uncontrollable impulse to *rush up trees and burst into song :* and you can't *stop it :* and it's *catching :* and there is only *one* cure : and it's *shooting.*

The Thrush

BIT VI

HUNTING ON THE HORSE

CHAPTER I

JOINING THE PACK

Mr. Saltena : ' I am not a gentleman, as they
say.'
Lord Clincham : ' Have some whisky ! '
The Young Visiters.

WHEN you have been ' hacking about ' for
two or three seasons, i.e. knickering and
knackering about the estate kicking pedes-
trians and other cluttering nuisances out of the way,
the local people will begin to alarm you by asking
whether you are not " coming out with hounds."

This is not a disease like coming out in spots, so
there is no need to gallop home and examine yourself
in the glass : your neighbours are merely trying to ask
you in a tactful way whether you are too mean or just
too cowardly to join the local Foxhounds and go
' Ahunting ' as it is technically called.

It is a most important moment in the career of a
horseman. Now is the time when you must decide
once and for all, are you really a g*ntl*m*n ? Because
if you are, then you have got to go out with hounds.
As Col: Numnah-Smith says, ' *The Englishman who
will not hunt is either a coward or a miser ; in either case
he is one of the two, if not both, and a cad to boot* '.

70

So unless you have the desperate courage of a Saltena and are prepared to say ' I am afraid I can't come out hunting, because as a matter of fact I'm rather a cad ' —and then bend over for the local people to boot you— you will be obliged to apply to the local Master of Fox-hounds for permission to join his Pack.

Enclose a recent photograph and a statement of your pedigree and if possible a warrant that you are free for the moment from foot-and-mouth disease, farcy, and E.S. (Webster's disease).   In due course you will receive a handsome pink membership card denoting that your application has been successful and that you have been ' Entered to Fox ' as the term is, and requesting you to present yourself at the next Meet ' For the purpose of Hunting The Fox the Whole Fox and nothing but the Fox, So Whelp you Pink '.   Frame this card and hang it over your fire-place next to the

coloured prints of ' The Moonlight Steeplechase ', and
then fling yourself into an arm-chair and contemplate
your good fortune.

Be careful not to fling the card into an arm-chair in
your excitement and hang yourself up over the fire-
place ; in fact do not get excited at all.   There is an
idea that people are expected to be very nervous when
first starting to hunt, for fear of doing the wrong thing,
such as wearing the wrong Hunt buttons on their
breeches, putting their boots on back to front, or
galloping over young greenhouses.   But there is no
need to worry (leave that to Hounds).   You will
find that Hunting Etiquette will all be explained to
you without the slightest hesitation by senior members
of the Hunt.

Indeed there is a special Official called the Master of
the Field whose business is to make beginners feel at
home by engaging them in sporting conversation.
Usually he will begin considerately with some easy
sporting questions such as ' Who-taught-*you*-to-ride-
to-hounds-Sir ? ' or, in more intimate style, ' Ever Seen
Young Grass Before ? '

Later on during the heat of the chase he will probably
show an even keener interest in your parentage and
upbringing, and ask some questions of a more technical
nature such as ' What the * ! ** ! * ! * ! * ? '

There are few things more touching in the world of
sport than the way old hands (and even old hounds)
will suddenly go off left-handed in full cry and sacrifice
a whole lot of breath and even sport, merely in order
to address a few technical words of advice to a complete
stranger.

Nor need you be alarmed by wild wives' tales and

old goose stories about the fearful *jumps* to be taken, the ' *bull-finches*,' ' *oxers* ', ' *gaspers* ', ' *double-chaffinches* ', ' *tom-tits* ', etc. Nearly all these dangerous obstacles have now been taken down and replaced by neat enclosures of pasturised-steel wire.

CHAPTER II

PREPARE TO HUNT

DURING summer the hunter (the horse, not you, Sir) is usually potted out to grass in paddocks, where it becomes quite stupid and docile and covered with flies and therefore doesn't count ; but as winter approaches hunters are taken back into stables and stuffed with wild oats to make them fierce and unmanageable and therefore worth riding to hounds.

So when the great day comes and you order out your moth-ridden grey dunlop you will find that your studgroom has not only worked it up into its primeval state (or ' condition ') of wildness but rendered it even more unreasonable, unrideable, etc., by scaffolding its neck with a tremendous variety of unwonted rigging and unwanted ratlines designed to help you control it at all its various paces. You will find that the baffle-rein or throttle which seemed so simple, and so single, when you were just hocking and plock-plocking about the roads has been entwined and entwangled with special standing martingales, running farthingales, and starting, stopping and stumbling nightingales.

And that the saddle has been entirely jungled up with special swingles and surcingles and super-swindle-trees,

so that if you pull the wrong farthingale or single out
the wrong swindlestrap, you will find yourself jingling,
and juggling and jumbling about in a most unsee-
worthy manner.

Your stud-groom will expect you to be frantically
bucked with all these gadgets. Don't worry, you'll not
disappoint him.[1]

* * *

You yourself will also have to turn out in quite a
new sort of kit—white leather breeches (so smart, and *so*
water-proof), black boots with washable pink celluloid
collars on them, a hunting-silk (or wire-haired top-hat),
a specially strangling kind of hunting-cravat (or
laughing-stock as it is called), a pair of white hunting-
gloves knitted out of white hunting string, and above
all a long Melberry-red tail-coat (dinner-jacket only, for
cub-hunting), which is called your Hunting Pink and
is the reason why a true Leicestershire Man always ends
a letter ' Hoping this finds you in the Pink as it leaves
me at present '.

On the other hand you will have to make up your
mind to do without a few things. If your are artistic
and wear a Bloomsbury beard (in Leicestershire they
laugh at beards and call them ' Belvoirs ') you will have
to shave that off or it will get entwingled in your startin-
gale, caught up in bull-finches, nested in by badgers,
etc., and might even result in the Pack *losing their fox*.

Similarly you had better do without the mane and
tail of your heiffer or bullion, and any other hair on it
which you might possibly hold on by. Holding on is

[1] The buck-royal, or Regency buck, is certain to materialize
before long.

despised by hunting-men, so put temptation **out of** your way by having your hunter ' cropped and crupped ', or ' hogged and hanked ' ; i.e., completely manxed at both ends.

Another thing you will have to drop is the definite article ; the word ' the ' is anathema to hunting-men

' Belvoir '

and if you are caught referring to *The* Hounds or in fact using the word ' the ' at all, once the Hunt is Up, it will be all up with you, too ; you will be immediately Entered to Horse-pond and later your Hunt buttons will be publicly hogged off and you will be chivvied and tantivvied out of the Pack.

NOTE :—Lady beginners, or ' novices ', are allowed (not unnaturally) to draw a veil over their faces. Men beginners are not allowed to take the veil (except in the V.W.H.), as it is maddening for the older members of the Pack when they cannot see what is going on beyond the veil, but can only hear the teeth chattering.

In conclusion let us acknowledge that there is no nobler sight than a hunting-man well turned-out, with his toes well turned-in and his horse well turned-off at the mane, and his own head completely turned-about with self-admiration and Press Photographers and anxiety not to kick hounds more than is good for them.

As for the Hunting Woman, all the above applies to her, except that she is not allowed to be in the Pink at present ; what is more, if she turns out correctly and often enough, who knows but a girl might end up by marrying an M.F.H. (or at least an Earth-stopper), though we must confess that marriers, as well as harriers and even farriers, seem to be rapidly dying out in the Shires, and that a furrier from the Finsbury Country would very likely be a more useful kind of husband in the long run.

*   *   *

So much for your kit : now for your equipment. You will probably want to take lunch as you gallop along, so in addition to your breakfast, which you should stow neatly away in your hunting-stomach before starting, you will have some sandwiches strapped to the saddle by means of a leather sursandwich, and a long tubular flask filled with a special dynamic drug called *jumping-powder* which will enable you to overcome the Moment of Inertia mentioned in Bit IV, Chap. IV.

These are the most essential, but there are many other things which might prove useful, such as a Field-Dressing or *First Aid Outfit* (bandages, crutches, some wooden legs, etc.)—you need not bother about your horse as it carries splints, etc., neatly stowed away in its own legs; a *hunting-knife* (for having a cut at the fences, particularly the oak ones); *wire-cutters, bangalore torpedoes*, etc., for destroying enemy wire; *spare safety-pin* (for securing Fox's ' brush ' to saddle if fox bursts, or saddle to horse if girth bursts); some useful books of reference (say, Beckford, Baedeker, Hansard, Debrett and, above all, Bradshaw); a mackintosh apron (if the day is a regular soaker); and a second-flask if self happens to be a

' Bogged, befogged and benighted '

regular soaker); a second-horse in case first runs away at Meet,[1] some second-sight (for ' watching Hounds work '); a second-seat, and, of course, a bag of bread-crumbs, groundsel, etc. (for Hounds).

Finally you might want a map of England in case

[1] A horse which runs away at the Meet is called, quite rightly, ' A Quittor'.

you get lost in a ' Big Country ' ; some spare woollens in case you get benumbed, and a tent, camp-bed, camp-stool, camp-commandant, etc., in case you get thoroughly lost, bogged, befogged and benighted in a county where you happen to be hated.

CHAPTER III

MEET MESSRS HOUNDS

THE ' Meet ' is a word which dates from the primitive days when each member of the Hunt brought his own hound under his arm and the Master, when the correct moment arrived, went round shouting, ' Hounds, gentlemen, please ', whereupon the members handed over their hounds to the Master who counted them— to see how many he would have to give back at the end of the day—having first arranged them in couples, which, as everyone knows, makes things twice as easy to count.

It is quite different now. Hounds all live together in kennels (where they are wrapped in flannels, fed through funnels, etc.) and the Meet is a purely sociological function held preferably at the Mansion of some Heavy Subscriber (or Big Music, asyermightsay) who must have a good cellar (to prevent people galloping about shouting things like, ' One man's Meet is another man's poison ') ; and the chief point about a Meet is the serving of a rather manly drink called a syrup-cup (made of cherry-brandy and stirrup of figs), the result being that the Master is compelled to curtail the orgy after a few minutes (in order to prevent everybody getting Histerrupcups or the Blind Staggers) by going round shouting, 'Time, gentlemen, please!' in the usual way.

When served with this traditional potion, or even with the more medicinal substitute known as hunting-port, you will, of course, show your appreciation by cracking your whip, smacking your lips and executing a few volte-faces, demi-tasses and quasi-volcanoes on your dappled walnut gallion.

In fact you should enjoy the Meet. It is a pretty sight; before you is the stately Mansion with the stately butlers on the lawn serving impossible drinks and the sprightly housemaids on the roof taking impossible snapshots; behind and on every side are thousands of Rolls-Royces, charabancs, motor horse-vans, movietone-men, monoplanes, gossip-writers, insurance-agents. . . .

Friends are greeting you, which is undoubtedly nice, enemies are cutting you (with their cutting-whips), which (according to Freud) is undoubtedly Vice. . . .

The Meet, in short, is fairly easy; for instance, very few people actually *fall off* at the Meet—if you are still at a stage when you fall off at a standstill you had better follow the example of the many cautious riders whom you will notice remaining in their Rolls-Royces and not mounting at all till Hounds have moved off, if then.

But don't take things too much for granted. For one thing there is a certain amount of *conversation* to be performed, most of it of a rather *technical nature*, such as 'Mornin', Major', 'Fine mornin', Colonel', etc. Until you have mastered these terms, and also the knack of taking off your hunting-hat unnecessarily

in spite of the fact that it is tethered to you with black
hunting-string, you had better say nothing at all. For
instance, don't go up to the Master and ask if he has
won the toss or whether our side is hare or hounds;
and if you actually spot some Hounds in the middle
of the gay scene, don't say 'Mornin'' to them or,
indeed, talk to them pleasantly at all—it is *sacrilegious*
to talk to a Hound as if it were an ordinary nice dog,
in fact the highest praise you can get in the Shires is
to be known as 'a hard man to Hounds'. So be
stern to them (they will mostly be that way to you),

and, above all, don't let your horse paw them, or
gnaw them, or *sit on them* even for a moment (see
above, p. 66, Dog-spavins).

One way and another there is a good deal of Red
Tape at the Meet; much of it is actually tied on to

the horses' tails to warn you that they have recently been vaccinated and are liable to kick, and even if your own horse does not kick much, it is a good plan to tie some red tape on to it so that if it starts a fight with another horse it will be the other horse's fault. (If both horses are marked with red tape, you will just have to claim that you tied yours on first.)

This principle of *tying things on* can be expanded. It is a good thing to tie tape on to *all* the dangerous points of your horse and then no one can say they weren't warned. You could also tie warnings *on to yourself*, i.e. BRASS PLACARDS of various kinds reading TOTALLY DEAF, or HOPELESSLY STUPID, or QUITE OUT OF CONTROL, or even NOT QUITE A G*NTL*M*N, so that people will know what to do about you.

CHAPTER IV

MEET MASTER FOX

AT length the great moment arrives ; the Master of
The Fox-hounds, being now quite out of patience, is
shouting ' Time, gentlemen, please ' ; the Owner of the
Mansion, being now right out of hunting-port, is lower-
ing his Port-cullis ; the Master of The Field has noted
' 361 mounted enemy ' in his Field Service Pocket-
book ; and the Master of the Rolls' has entered ' 71
couple and 9 Blood Bentleys plus 43 chars-à-bancs ' in
his Wakefield Service Sprocket-book ; and in the midst
of all this, to the great despair of all but a few vulpicidal
maniacs, *Hounds are moving off*.

Follow the crowd to the covert-side, and *wind your
hunting-horn*, or beagle, over the right shoulder under
left arm-pit and back over to right elbow and for
Blood's sake not round horse's neck.

Now keep your eyes skinned for a Fox, and remember
if you see one you must *shout, halloo, tantootle*, and
tarradiddle for all you're worth.

Far away in the whin-bushes you hear (the) Hounds
(nearly forgot) whinneying, and even further away in
the spinney some more Hounds (dodged it) spinneying.
The rain (surely we mentioned that it has been raining
since yesterday-fortnight—come-Michaelmas ;. if not,
note it at once in your Mud-book), the rain descends in
torrents all down your neck and crop, and is rapidly
filling your long tubular boots.

Minutes pass. There is nothing you can do but
rehearse once more all your in-born knowledge about

the Fox ;—how cunning it is ; the way it wears *pads*
to protect it against rough-riders who descend to mere
hacking-about in the hunting-field, and a *brush* at the
back to efface its footprints in the mud as fast as it
makes them, and how its face is always a *mask*—so
that nobody can ever tell what it is thinking about.

Face is always a *mask*

And then what a little dandy is Master Fox ; the
quantity of *scent* he uses, for instance, especially on
damp, warm, fuggy days, and the way he dresses just
like the Hunt with a smart red coat and a white cravat
and little pink fox-gloves on his fingers . . . no wonder
all true sportsmen, ever since the days of Beau Pummel,
the famous hunting-dandy, raise their hats in silent
admiration on viewing a well-turned-out fox setting
out from the covert for a day's hunting ' with the cream
of the squires over the salt of the Earth '—as hunting-
writers say.

And yet even in the matter of scent the Varmint is
not to be relied on. Some days he deliberately *leaves
it behind* for Hounds and Huntsman to pick up as best
they can. On others he will suddenly throw it up
about ten feet in the air so that the Huntsman has to
lift Hounds to enable them to see where it has got to.

When you think of all the unnecessary trouble which

Foxes give the Hunt it is amazing how much sporting consideration is shown to them.

In fact, as opposed to Riding at which (as we have

Viewing well-turned-out fox

hinted) everything possible is done to make things disheartening for the rider, at Fox-hunting everything imaginable is done to make things easier and quicker for the Fox.[1] To give only one example, the Hunting Season begins with Cub-hunting when the Hunt puts itself to extraordinary inconvenience in order to be UP long before dawn, and goes round to the various coverts teaching young foxes to be up early, instead of

[1] The whole thing, as every stable-boy knows, was originally started at the Foxes' request (cf. Ed. II, Petition of Foxes—' For ye Abolition of Serf-riding and for more, and more speedier, Huntynge instedde '; 1324).

lousing about after their late nights with the chickens, and to dash out promptly into the Field when the Huntsman blows his horn; and above all, to *run straight.*

And yet, would you believe it, there are foxes which grow up to be 'Twisters' or 'Ringers' or 'Double-Crossers'—in fact just *Crooks.* These animal-cads

Has to lift Hounds

invariably try to spoil sport by 'doubling' without any warning in the middle of a run, i.e., by turning right round and charging the Hunt, thus compelling everyone to reverse suddenly and *gallop backwards* (a most uncomfortable gait).

Or else they suddenly 'go left-handed', when true sportsmen are expected to ride sideways and Hounds to run tied tail-to-tail, in order that everything should be fair for all. . . .

But hark forrard! What is that we see threshing and crashing around just inside the covert? It is the Huntsman himself who has dismounted and gone in to help Hounds find their fox. See how he lashes with his fox-whip at a thick fern-bed and shouts 'Leu out, you skulker! No loitering, now, you four-flushing son of a badger!' and other daring phrases. You may

Left-handed

depend on it there is an old grog-fox in that bush and that if he doesn't come out soon and show some sport the Master himself will be sent in to 'chop him in covert' with his little hatchet.

Meanwhile we may just have time to run through——

CHAPTER V

PAID SERVANTS OF THE HUNT

> 'Patience, and shuffle the Pack.'
> Old Spanish Hunting-Proverb.

To help him in his Superhuman task of showing sport (and defeating the Fox), the Master has not only his Hounds but also a number of Hunt Servants. That was one we saw in the covert—the Huntsman, whose job it is to find the fox and then hunt it.

Besides having a hard well-trained seat, a long sharp tongue and a cast in his eye the Huntsman must have all his senses very well developed. For instance, there is often a nasty *smell* of some sort in the covert and Hounds are sure to notice this and if it is a puzzling smell will get confused and start ' rioting ' and rotting about in all directions instead of looking for the fox. The Huntsman must be able to tell whether the nasty smell is a badger or a bad pheasant's egg and must *smell it first*, and so be able to warn Hounds and stop the rot.

The Huntsman must also know the names of all Hounds and Foxes[1] in his Country and is expected to show the Master which jumps are jumpable (by jumping them first).

But the most romantic Hunt servant is the *Earth-stopper*, whose job, however, is not quite so ambitious as it sounds, but consists mainly in trying *to prevent the Fox missing the enjoyment of the run by plunging down holes in the earth.*

The other servants are the First Whip and the Second Whip. In olden days the Huntsman did all the

[1] This is easy as all Foxes have the same name, i.e. ' Leonard '.

Whipping himself; that was too tiring, and nowadays he has these two great whopping little whipper-strappers to help him.

But hark, sideways! Here is the First Whip himself coming our way, his eye glued to the covert. Suddenly he unglues it with a skilful motion and with a horse cry of '*Gone Away!*' crashes through a cut-and-dried hedge and is gone!

Don't turn to your friend Lord Londlaird and say, ' What a pity he got so impatient and went away—just aş I was beginning to like him ', but cram your first-hat well down on your head, shout Whoohoop! or Whip-whip-whooray! and gallop cautiously after the First Whip at a rapid trot.

As you go, His Londship will doubtless be glad to explain to you that one of the most technical and clever things a Fox does is to ' go away '; and that very few other animals would have the *sang-froid*, when their homes were suddenly invaded by 20 couple of Hounds and half-a-couple of smelly old huntsman on all fours, to just ' go away ', like that. . . .

The Second Whip's duty, he will go on to tell you, is to keep on *counting Hounds*, because towards the end of the day, when the Fox has used up all its scent, Hounds sometimes get bored and start going away, too. The Second Whip then pursues *them :* so if he meets you on his rounds and you are not busy, but, say, sitting in a ditch or resting on somebody else's laurels or rhododendrons, or wherever your strawberry-foal happens to have deposited you, don't just sit there saying nothing, but encourage the Second Whip with technical words of comfort : bark out ' Only just this minute a couple-and-a-half passed right under my

nose, blowing through the spinney right-handed ', or
' Only two minutes gone, I saw half-a-couple of skirters
feathering on their rullocks stern-foremost down
Dingle's Ten-acre '.

Remember, the next noblest thing to talking intelli-
gently about Horses is barking unintelligibly about
Hounds.

CHAPTER VI

UNPAID DITTOES

So much for the paid servants of the Hunt. But there
are also two others, unpaid for, whom you must never
forget—The Master of the Fox Hounds himself and the
Hunt Secretary. The Master is not only unpaid but
used formerly to pay for everything connected with
the Hunt and still pays for practically everything else
within a radius of 30 miles of the kennels.

He, as every pedestrian knows, is responsible for the
Whole Affair. If the Fox runs riot that is his fault ;
the weather, the wire, the bad scent, the charabancs
and you—all his fault. No wonder he is not only
vulpicidal at all times but even a little homicidal at
odd moments. And no wonder that it is the proudest
moment (or Hippopotheosis) of your life when you
are singled out of the whole Field for the special
distinction of being bloodied, as it is called, by The
Master.

The Hunt Secretary's business is to collect sub-
scriptions, and take off his cap to strangers at the Meet
and not to put it on again till he has seen two guineas
in it.

Avoid the Hunt Secretary, through modesty and so on, if you like and on no account get hysterical and start putting guineas into *all* the hats that are taken off to you at the Meet—but remember that the second proudest moment in your horse-life will come when, after hunting for your County for three years without being noticed, you are finally ' capped ' by the Hunt Secretary and know that you have now got your County colours.   Then you can start taking off *your* hat, with a two-pound look, to any Strangers you see at the Meet—after all you never know . . . especially if they don't know much either. . . .

CHAPTER VII

GONE AGLEY !

'The Unspeakable in pursuit of the Uneatable.'
O. WILDE.

WHEN last seen you were galloping cautiously after the Fox at a rapid trot.   How have you been getting on ?   Or have you been falling off ?   And if so, again, how have you been getting on ?   Have you been feeling the blood of your ancestors coursing, cursing, etc., through your veins, reins, brains, etc. ?   Or have you just been feeling a complete cad ?

On the contrary, remembering the advice given in all the textbooks, you have selected an experienced rider to follow—Mrs. Foxer, perhaps, who knows the country like the back of her hand (and Egad, they're alike) ; or old Admiral Mainbrace, who knows the game so well that he sees plenty of Hounds (more than there are, sometimes) and yet hardly ever has to take a jump.

You have chosen the Navigator ? Good, somehow we thought you would—and now we are all thudding down a lane in the wake of the Admiral, going astutely at right angles to the line the Fox has taken. . . .

You will remember this lane : all hunting novices know it. We shall see more of it, swallow some of it, and in the end take most of it back home on us. . . .

At the end of the lane a countryman with a manure-cart raises his hat (out of rustic respect for the Admiral or possibly out of scientific reverence for manure) and cries, ' Fox gone by here five seconds ago ! '

' Not our Fox ', shouts the Admiral astutely, and signs for silence. *Far away we hear the faint note of a hunting-horn.*

Turning our horses we canter astutely up the lane, and at a sign from Admiral M. halt and strain our ears for a view.

Far away we glimpse the faint whistle of a shunting-engine.

Reversing our horses we gallop sternly down the lane. This time the man does not raise his hat. We throat-lash him. . . .

At the end of the lane the Admiral sighs for a drink. . . . *Far away he hears the pubs opening.* . . . Without waiting to reverse our horses we gallop stern-foremost up the lane. The countryman hides astutely under the manure-cart. . . .

* * *

As we pass him for the 18th time, the countryman suddenly stands up and holloas in desperation, ' Fox gone by here five hours ago '.

At a sign from the Admiral we dismount : the man is entered to manure-cart.

Suddenly Admiral M. has one of his well-known bursts of hunting genius. Draining his second-flask with a skilful motion, he pushes his horse up a bank. We dismount and push ours up, too. Before us is a stretch of open country. The great grass pastures are intoxicating, especially for cows, but Admiral M. warns us not to take too much out of our horses at first. After a short consultation we decide just to take the teeth out, for safety's sake, and to let our horses have their heads for the time being : the animals are by now much thinner, so in addition we tighten the girths. At a sign from the Admiral we drain our third-flasks, and pin our breeches to the saddle with our spare safety-pins.

Scarcely have we done so when Hounds crash into view. It is a sight for sore withers ! The Huntsman blowing his hunting-horn ; The Master blowing his hunting-nose ; the ' first flight '—Tom-sawyers to a man and even some Melberry Fans on visit from the Shires. . . . In front of them is a blind double-oxer, staked, half-timbered and faced with rough-cast concrete, with an open ditch to-them and the great Geoffrey Brook yawning on the further side. A frightful crash ! Two are down but both men are on their feet, still holding their horses ; further along two more men, still on their horses but both holding their heads ; in the next field we can see three men on their heads still holding their feet ; and at the bottom of the Brook several more men, still holding their breath. . . .

Clenching our teeth we prepare to die in the first ditch.

But a sign from our leader arrests us.

'Not our Hunt', says the Admiral quietly, and turning back-handed, plunges astutely into The Lane. . . .

* * *

But now our blood is up, we are determined not to follow any more red Admirals but to pursue the Fox personally—any Fox—with any Hunt—we will even pay another two guineas if caught by another Hunt Secretary. Our blood, clearly, is just about boiling over. . . .

Far away in the distance an old unclipped farmer is holding up a turnip to show that the Fox has gone to seed. Clenching our second-teeth we fly over the brook at the nearest bridge and are up just in time to see the Huntsman casting Hounds one by one into a dew-pond.

Now they are out and hunting their Fox gamely round and round the great bowl of marshland known since King Arthur's day as the Devil's Sponge-bag.

Yonder he goes ! There he is, only two fields in front, and heading apparently for Manchester. And here are we, only two miles behind, and heading, eventually, for disaster. Hark innards ! We would dearly like to eat our sandwiches, or even the bark off our saddle-trees, but the pace is too good. The Hunt Secretary is capping us on again. Another two guineas—one almost prays for a cheque.

Ha ! What now ? Yelps ! Wither away ! Hounds have got their heads up, and this has got the Huntsman's back up. Some sheep have charged over the line and scored a try in a corner of the Field (three points). The Master is cursing his weight, and throwing

his horse about ; he has made *his* point (in fact he has
said everything and is now running his foils over stale
ground).

*But far away in the distance a man is standing on a
mole-hill holding up a badger to show that the Fox has
gone aground.*

Hurry ! We must be in at the earth ! It is our
earthright. Meanwhile we have got our girth-wrong :
but no matter, we are up with Hounds now, and there
is time to ride at anchor a minute and look around
and *assess the Grief.* What a sight ! Col: A. has been
strangled by his laughing-stock ; Lady B. has swallowed
her veil and is dying of string-halt ; the Rev. C., who
is suffering from Loose-girths, Leviticus, Numnahs,
etc., has ridden the last three miles upside-down
underneath his horse. . . .

But Amen to all that, things are beginning to move
again. The second-terrier has unearthed the Fox. A
pedestrian has headed it and the First Whip has, quite
rightly, beheaded the pedestrian. Hurry ! We are
falling behind again. Steady ! We have fallen off in
front again. Meanwhile Dusk is falling all over the
place. . . .

We are running now left-footed in our top-boots
across a ploughed field. We are grasping now for our
second foils and running-through a couple of pedes-
trians ; we are gasping now for our second-breath and
slithering on our rullocks stern-foremost down Ding-
Dong Dell. *Far away in the distance a policeman is
holding up the charabangs to show that he is Master of
the Situation.* . . .

But there is good news ! A woman with a bicycle
has seen our Fox ; an old man in a tricycle has headed

our horse ; but the horse has got the bicycle between its teeth and the woman has retaliated by savaging our sursandwich ; she has told the First Whip that the old man in the tricycle is not a gentleman. . . . Our horse (there are several of us on it now, including Capt. X who lost his horse at the Meet, and Maj. Y who drowned his in the Dewpond, and Professor Z who never had a horse in his life and now thinks he is having a night-mare) crashes through a ten-barred iron gate and we find ourselves once more in The Lane. . . .

Hark harkwards now ! The Huntsman is blowing the Dead March in Saul ; Hounds have caught and killed the man with the manure-cart ; but The Master is not satisfied and has gone away, heading for Birmingham, with a bit of the Fox between his teeth. The woman without the bicycle is still foiling the old man, with the tricycle, who, so far as we can see in the failing light, is still not quite a gentleman.

The Sun sets. . . .

Far away in the distance a man is standing on a windmill, holding up a night-light to show that the Fox has now definitely gone to bed. . . .

Hounds and all, we settle down in The Lane and have a good cry (Eheu ! Oyoyoy ! Gotterdammerung !)

*   *   *

What a Day ! What a Run ! A 3-mile Point and 76 miles as Hounds ran riot. And now (what a nuisance) we have lost ourselves. Must we erect our tent and shackle our froth-ridden bay gudgeon to a telegraph pole ? But honk ! Is not that our second-Rolls approaching, leaving a faint scent, axle-high ? Yes, it is Rawlplug himself, our thrusty second-chauffeur who has followed the Hunt all day by devious by-passes and is now approaching in second-gear with respectful toots upon his Royce horn. In a tricicle we have sold our horse to the woman without the bicycle and are purring homewards to Dingley Hall. . . .

And now come the best, the only unfailing pleasures of the chase—our blood-hot bath, our gin with our bitters, our dinner with Our Betters; the Port of our ancestors and the talk of our exploits and particularly, of course, the exploits of the Pack. That was, naturally, now that we come to drink it over, what we enjoyed most of all—*Watching Hounds Work*. What tremendous fun it was; how eagerly we watched them lathering on the chop as we went thrusting gamely at that half-open hunting-gate, how shrewdly we viewed old 'Faithful' speaking to the scent and young 'Mouthful' stopping to speak to a dead rabbit, how anxiously we marked 'the ladies' lifting the skirt to heel and the skirters heeling the Fox out of the scrub, as we crashed our knee on the gate post and shouted 'Sorry, sir!' into the nostrils of the Bloodmaster's big bay mastodon. . . .

Or again, as we plunged full-yoicks down Cropneck Scarp with the Joint-Mistress's iron-grey bludgeon blowing white-hot smoke between the tails of our Pink, how gaily we let the reins drop and raised our field-glasses to *make sure* that Hounds were carrying a good head of hare; and how gravely we tapped our tuning-fork and checked the Music when Hounds burst into psalm No. 301 as they ran past Foxminster Cathedral.

And there were those long glorious hours in the second-lane, when the pace wasn't quite such a scream and we could watch Hounds really intimately: that time, for instance, when we cast ourselves so knowingly into a hawthorn bush to get a better view of ' Jovial ' babbling on the slug, and that other time when our horse, ' up to every turn of the game ', climbed the old spreading Elm-tree to let us see ' Garrulous ' fling his tongue at a twisting mangy vixen and miss her by a mare's-breath. . . .

BIT VII

PUNTING ON THE HORSE

> ' After all, at the Day of Judgment, what will be
> the odds ? '   LORD CLINCHAM.
>
> ' Tishy, Tishy, all fall down ! '
>   Old Manton Nursery Rhyme.

SOMETIMES when there aren't many people at table and everyone has told everyone else the same story about how they watched Hounds working the Fox to death while the old mare leapt the ' Flying Scotsman ', one can for a change start joking in a boastful sort of way about all the ' fivers,' ' ponies ', ' monkeys ' and ' cool thous ' one has been losing lately on the Turf.

(The best people understand at once that one didn't let all this money drop out of one's trouser-pocket while lolling around on the Downs or one of the few other places in England where one is not definitely warned off the Grass, but lost it in the noblest possible way by punting it on to the wrong horse.)

Very well, then : you had better make your position in society absolutely secure by losing a few millions ; and you will no doubt be relieved to know that as opposed to riding on the Horse everything is made as easy as possible for beginners who want to try losing on the 'osses. For instance, unlike the Huntsman, the

Puntsman does not need to have a good pair of hands or a grand seat : all he needs is a Grand Stand and a good pair of field-glasses.

Indeed, he does not even need to go to race-courses at all : anyone can learn all he wants to about betting from one of the correspondence-courses conducted by well-known Commission Agents.

You, however, will wish to do the thing in style ; so to begin with you will have to go in a Racing Special train full of card-sharpeners who will cheat you frightfully at ' Racing-Demon ' and ' Beggar-my-neighbour ' and won't allow you to go nap for a minute.

When you reach the course you will purchase a race-card (1s. outside the gate, second-hand ; 6d. inside, new) which will tell the age, weight, colour and pedigree of the Clerk of the Scales, the First Lord of the Totalisator (or To'sun) and other officials ; and your first impression of the Meeting will be that you have strolled into a vast race-paper basket littered knee-deep with midday editions, race-cards, cigarette cards, betting slips and all the scrum of the earth, not to mention the scurf of humanity—tipsters and tapsters, bookies and crookies, tick-tackers and pick-pocketeers. . . .

Clutch your monkeys tightly to your breast-pocket and hurry past into the betting ring. Here the game is evidently one of racing pandemonium : bookies are roaring ' Six-to-four-the-Field ', orange vendors are howling ' Four-p'nce-ha'p'ny-the-bag ', ice-cream merchants are ice-screaming nineteen-to-the-dozen, and everyone seems to have so much to say to no one in particular that you hardly dare interrupt Mr. Ike Williams to ask him what time the 2.30 starts, or whether ' backing both-ways ' is the same as ' heads-I-

win-tails-you-lose ', or which horse would be the best
to bet on, or even which race he expects to welsh on. . . .

In the end you decide to punt your money into the
Tote, because it never welshes, but whichever horse
you back you are almost certain to lose because there
is such a lot of white-tape and back-scratching, and
objecting about a horse-race ; so even if your horse
' arrives ' officially on the course it may get its back
officially scratched and refuse to start, and even if it
starts it may go off the rails and arrive unofficially in
the Grand Stand, which doesn't count, and even if it
comes in first your jockey may object that he was
bored by the whole thing from start to finish and refuse
to weigh-in, and your monkey will die after all.

Yes, it hardly matters really which horse you back.
An enormous majority of them will lose the race anyway, so if you want to boast of your losses afterwards
you have a pretty large choice. But make up your mind
beforehand *which way* you want to bet—whether to *win*
or to *lose*. Some people (especially when backing the
favourite) *back it both ways*, i.e., to win *and* to lose :
which is pretty safe because the odds are usually *on* the
favourite instead of against it, so that you stand to lose
more if the horse loses than you stand to win if it wins,
and thus, if it wins, you win less than you would have
lost if it had been the other way round and had run
backwards, or both-ways, while if the horse loses, then
you lose too because you betted the bookie you would
(unless the horse won). You do follow that, don't you ?

But on the whole it is not advisable to back the
favourite : *it carries too much weight*. What with the
jockey, and all the stones they hang on its saddle, and
the thousands of shirts of the male backers and the

millions of skirts of the female backers and all the bloomers made by wire and mail on it, the favourite usually gets left behind at the start, or ‘lost in the Post’, as the saying is.

By far the most sporting thing to do is to put your shirt on an Outsider—and here again you should put it on *both ways*, i.e., outside-in *and* inside-out ; though it will probably scratch either way. . . .

But the bells are already ringing in the bar for you to take your seat. Horses are beginning to canter past from paddock to post. They are pulling their jockeys and trying to get ‘off’. (Later some of the jockeys will be getting off and trying to pull their horses.) And there goes your Outsider ! Pirouetting sideways down the course ! He is wearing White, with Scarlet cross-belts (2nd class), Cerise breeches, hooped, with tassels, and boots reversed ; cap, Tangerine halved and gutted with White pips, etc., etc.

The race is a Maiden Selling Plate (5 forelocks) for graylings (5 lb. and upwards), and ghillies (50 years and downwards), the winner to be sold by auction (50 guelders upwards), the losers to be drowned by suction (50 fathoms downwards)

And now they’re off ! The great moment has come ; you have almost lost your first monkey. What a sight ! The man in front of you is wearing a Moss-green overcoat with Yellow seams, and Moth-bitten trousers with Black checks, Chocolate collar and cuffs, Amber diamonds, Puce boots, and Orange cap reversed. That is all you can see of the race ; but what a sight !

And now everyone is waving umbrellas in the air and shouting. Bookies are beginning to welsh wholesale ; Tipsters, as they promised, are beginning to eat their hats piecemeal: suddenly the ghillies flash past and are gone; and the race is over; and everyone is boasting and laughing and chaffing about the monkeys and donkeys and sea-elephants they lost on the favourite. . . .

* * *

But enough. It is unnecessary for you to describe all these picturesque details over the Port: all you need do is to mention casually that you have been punting heavily and losing handsomely, and to hint darkly that you propose to push the old grey mare ' over the sticks ' at Elstree next month. And you might perhaps slip in an occasional mention of the great classic races in the Calendar, such as ' The Oats ' or ' The Thousand Pities ', and tell them how you hired a tank last August to go to the Derby and saw the best of the race from the corner of Tottenham Court Road, or what horse you fancy for ' The Cezarewitch '.

But bewarewitch ! Don't go on too long, or your host will raise the red flag over the decanter and ' object ' to you on the ground that you are an Outsider and doped, anyway, now; and that it is time you romped home in a taxi and went to ground in the bolster.

* * *

Finally, if you are sufficiently mean and unsportsmanlike to try deliberately to *make* money by Punting on the Horse, don't imagine that you can do it by ' studying form ' or any nonsense of that sort—much less by studying the Noble Animal, which has *nothing to do with betting at all*. What you want is a ' system '

And the truth is that there is only one ' system ' which *works invariably :* it is world-wide, and globe-ridden, and is recommended by all the most reliable swindlers, thimble-riggers and pecksniffs : and it works like this :

Suppose the race in question is at 2.30, say at Doncaster ; the Swindler, say at Birmingham, rings up a bookie at Doncaster, say at 2.35, and asks him which horse has won the 2.30. And the bookie says ' Bellerophon ', or something like that. Then the Trickster says, keeping quite calm, ' O, thanks—well, I'll lay a cool thou' on Bellerophon for the 2.30 ', and the bookie says ' Bellerophon ! ' (or something like that) ' It's too late : your bet doesn't count '. Then the Cheatster, who *always keeps his watch six minutes slow,* says ' On the contrary, my good bookie : it's only 2.29 at Birmingham, so it's O.K.' And so it counts, and the Backster makes a lot of money, say about 33 cool thous, and he can't be found out because he gets *lots of witnesses* (who are all picaroons and artful dodgers like himself) to look at his watch while he is telephoning, Bellerophoning, etc., and this establishes an *alibi* (American : *attaboy ;* Yiddish : *ichabod*) and the Law can't make head or tail of it and he gets away with it and does it again and again and again, and if you ask him about it he just says ' Well, that's my system, and I stick to it '.

And so now you know.

BIT VIII

THE HORSE IN HISTORY AND LITERATURE

CHAPTER I

WRONG ORIGINS OF THE HORSE

Dawn of Horse, Horses of Dawn, etc.

WHATEVER may be the origin of the various pads and prads, palfreys and pranceys, rounceys and bounceys with which romantic literature has become piebald, we must emphasize at once that the real Noble Animal has *not* evolved, as the Ancients evidently thought, from any monstrous flying-fish or chimerical *bird*. There are genuine horses

on every page of Handley Cross, but we never saw a horse yet that was a genuine cross with Handley Page.

We cannot therefore commend at all such mythical animals as the *winged Pegasoss* (by Poseidon out of Gorgon's Blood), which rapped the summit of Mount Helicon with its forefoot, thus causing the thrushful

Greek horses or chevaux-de-frieze,
with too many legs

Hippocrene (the blue, the blushful Keats, etc.). While as for all the other Greek horses, they seem either to have had *far too many legs* to be the progenitors of anything handier than a Centipede, or else to have been just rather *disgusting*, like the ones in the memorable Augean Stables which *hadn't been cleaned for forty years* (*Stinky-pinky parlez-vous.* Old Greek chorus).

Nor are we concerned here with the transient and nebulous Eoss (which was *A Roarer*, anyway, as old Jorrocks knew) or with the even more ancient and fabulous Sea-'oss (see 'oss in Fig. X), but solely with

the genesis of the genuine Gee'oss of our own day—
which you will find fully and unanswerably depicted
in Chapter II.

Fig. X

CHAPTER II

EVOLUTION OF THE GENUINE GEE'OSS

A GREAT deal of credit must be given to the famous
Geologists who succeeded in evolving the genuine
Gee'oss from the very Unnatural Selection of 'osses
depicted on the right. And also to the great Painters
who have sent it sartorious, happy and glorious on its
way. No one, not even Capt. Pontoon, would deny
that, whatever may be said of the first 200,000 years,
the Breed, during the last two hundred, has made
great strides, and, though now practically exstinct, is
running its race out magnificently.

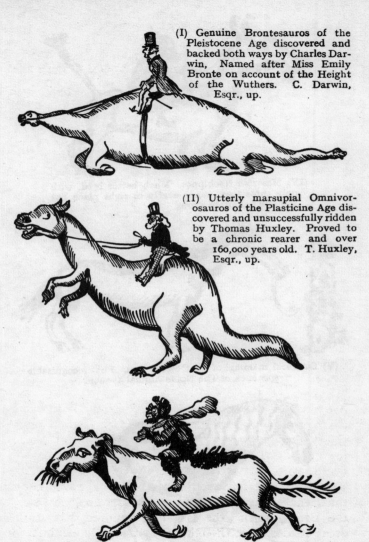

(I) Genuine Brontesauros of the Pleistocene Age discovered and backed both ways by Charles Darwin. Named after Miss Emily Bronte on account of the Height of the Wuthers. C. Darwin, Esqr., up.

(II) Utterly marsupial Omnivorosauros of the Plasticine Age discovered and unsuccessfully ridden by Thomas Huxley. Proved to be a chronic rearer and over 160,000 years old. T. Huxley, Esqr., up.

(III) Protozoic Preposteros. A very low-bred animal with seven toes, no withers and the wrong kind of tail. Note also mane in wrong place.

(IV) Mesozoic Neohippos. Much better bred, with only three toes; mane nearly in right place but tail still definitely wrong.

(V) Cursorial mammal of the Obscene Age. First recognisable specimen of The Noble Animal as such.

(VI) Early horse of the Must'ang Dynasty (China). Very valuable and docile (a child could break it).

(VII) **Fifteenth Century Palfrey** or **Mediæval Clothes Horse.** In the picture the animal is shown pricking-forth In Search of Merry England.

(VIII) **Seventeenth Century Prancey** or **Roly-Pony,** invented by Velasquez and useful for caracoling, equestrian statues and other bulbous amenities.

(IX) **Final result** or **Apotheosis of the Horse.** Perfectly bred animal ridden by perfectly bred vegetable. The whole thing perfectly parallel and perfectly impossible.

CHAPTER III

HISTORIC HORSES

> ' Alexander had a hoss
> Which he called Bucephalos.'
> *Eton Punting Song.*

THERE are, as a matter of fact, if anyone likes to count them, just about as many horses as there are people in History ; King Solomon alone, for instance, had 10,000 horses as well as all the wives and thingummies. We regret to say, however, that most of the really memorable horses were in the nature of freak horses, full of dam-circus-tricks, and we have therefore thought it best to dock the list of them as short as possible.

CATALOGUE OF HISTORIC HORSES

Wooden Horse of Troy (see Fig. XI). Shapeless pot-bellied brute, revealing (*a*) abysmal ignorance of Greeks concerning horses (see Wrong Origins, above) ; they apparently thought the place for the horseman was *inside* the horse ; (*b*) first classic example of a *Gift Horse* (*Timeo Danaos et dona ferentes*) ; the Trojans should have looked *in its belly*. (A *casus belli*, asyermightsay.)

Bucephalos. Apart from its name (see Eton Punting Song, above) nothing is known of this sententious animal except that it used to sit down to enable

Alexander to mount it, or possibly through a mistaken idea that it could be put into Latin more easily in this posture.

Emperor Colicula's horse. A trencher-fed creature; drank wine out of a golden plate (v. clever). Colicula, recognising frankly that he himself was quite devoid of horse-sense, made it not only a Consul but also a Priest, probably on account of its wine-born knowledge of the Colic for the day.

Rustum's horse. Had the unusual name of *Rusk*. Influenced by this, made cakes in the sand by weeping on it (see poem by Matthew Arnold). This is of course very difficult to do as well as to believe and an instance of poetic nuisance.

Sharetz. The piebald property of King Marko of Old Serbia : chosen by him as being the only horse which he couldn't swing round his head by the tail. (Very selective.) Knelt down in battle to enable enemy cavalry to charge right over King Marko without touching him. Meanwhile Marko tent-pegged the enemy from below. (Very spectacular.)

Banks's Horse. Famous Steeple-chaser with circus-tricks. Climbed the spire of St. Paul's Cathedral. Excommunicated by Pope for trying same trick at St. Peter's, Rome.

Bayard. A very long mediæval horse which got longer and longer as more and more people got on to its back (at intervals, Roncevalles, etc.).

Weston Super-Mare. Largest horse on record. Stood 23 hands and drinks all round after winning the Schneider Cup at Troy-weights in 1801.

Marengo. Napoleon's horse ; had silver snuff-boxes instead of feet, so that Napoleon always rode on the snuffle. All English regimental messes now possess one of these silver snuff-boxes; Marengo was therefore evidently another of those horses with *too many feet*. 'Snuffofthis.

Fig. XI. Casus belli

CHAPTER IV

HOW TO WRITE ABOUT THE HORSE

I. POETRY

> ' To saddle, skiddaddle, boot horse and away ! '
> ROBERT BROWNING.

UNLIKE Nightingales, Skylarks and Mice—the Horse has never been the subject of any absolutely desperate literary emotion. No one apparently has felt an uncontrollable impulse, on opening the stable door, to shout ' Hail to thee, blithe fillet '.

The fact is that really soul-shattering poetry of the kind which begins with unbridled interjections like

' O ' or ' Ah God ! ' is not inspired by The Noble Animal (especially if its uncomfortable motion is recollected in tranquillity). On the contrary, verses about the horse usually begin with the more bestial ejaculation—

' Ho '.

This should be followed by a mark of interjection, thus—

' Ho ! '

to express the horseman's surprise at finding himself writing a poem at all.

After that, the poem should get into its stride at once : e.g.

> ' Ho ! Toss me my beaver and saddle my mare ! '

or, in a circumstance of great agitation,

> ' Ho ! Saddle my beaver and toss me my mare ! '

But if, by any chance, when you have written the word ' Ho ! ' nothing seems to follow naturally after it, it is permissible to cross out ' Ho ! ' and begin again with ' Come ! '

This should always introduce some great feat of condescension on the part of the writer, usually the giving away of a tremendous ' only-the-best-people-are-in-on-this ' kind of secret, such as

> ' Come ! I'll show you a country that none can surpass ',

or, better still—

> ' Come ! I'll tell you a story I trust you all know '.

And after that all you require is a good manly refrain like ' A rum one to saddle, a bad one to boot ! ' and a long list of rhymes for boot, such as hoot, toot,

boot, brute, boot, flute, Marquis of Bute, Marchioness
of Boot, etc., and with the help of a whisky-and-soda
or two the poem is practically made.

BOOTS AND SADDLES

One way and another it will be seen that poems
about the Horse are always *tremendously urgent ;*
plenty of things are ' flung ' and ' tossed ' with never
a moment to be lost—though there is usually just time
to drain off a bumper or two to King Charles, or to
bump off a pedestrian or two (Pym and such carles).

And there is a good deal of special *leathery technique.*
This, as hinted above, is largely a matter of Boots and
Saddles, which ought both to be injected at intervals
(by a Veterinary Surgeon if necessary) throughout the
poem ; and it is also essential to *suggest* (without, of
course, actually introducing) some shockingly *devil-
may-care swear words.* The best way to bring it off is
to end one of the unimportant lines with a word like
' crammed ', or ' hammed '—e.g.

> *' The port's in the holster, the sandwich is hammed ',*

or,

> *' The fetlocks are padlocked, the forelocks are jammed ' ;*

Then, quite suddenly, when nobody suspects what
is going to happen, you bring the passage to a crashing
culmination with

> *' Boots and saddles ! To horse and be d———— ! '*

When you have done that and left your readers
trying to work out what the devil-you-meant, you
should count the lines in the stanza (or furlong) and if
you don't think that there are quite enough yet, you

can always add with a quite unexpected spasm (or
spavin) of inspiration (after another quite unexpected
whisky-and-soda or two)—

> ' *Boots and saddles ! !   To horse and be d——d ! !* '

or, once more, if you think they still haven't quite
got it—

> ' BOOTS AND SADDLES ! ! !   TO HORSE AND BE D*MN*D ! ! ! '

But it is unusual, not to say unsportsmanlike, to
repeat the same line more than *three times* consecutively.
Even the Best People will begin to get sick of it in the
end and to suspect that you are not *writing quite
straight*.

But in case you are not yet convinced of the extreme
urgency of equestrian poetry, we shall now quote one
of the most strikingly urgent poems in the English
language—written, although even a polished horseman
can hardly be asked to remember this, by Robert
Browning—who, if no great horseman, was at least,
as you shall see, a rare one to gallop and a rum one to
follow.

It is entitled—

HOW I BROUGHT THE GOOD NEWS FROM AIX TO GHENT

(or Vice Versa)

and runs (or rather gallops) roughly as follows : we
quote from memory (having no boots of reference at
hand) :

> ' I sprang to the rollocks and Jorrocks and me,
>   And I galloped, you galloped, he galloped, we galloped all
>   three . . .
>   Not a word to each other ; we kept changing place,
>   Neck to neck, back to front, ear to ear, face to face ;

And we yelled once or twice, when we heard a clock chime,
" Would you kindly oblige us, *Is that the right time ?* "
As I galloped, you galloped, he galloped, we galloped, ye
  galloped, they two shall have galloped ; *let us trot.*

. . . .

I unsaddled the saddle, unbuckled the bit,
Unshackled the bridle (the thing didn't fit)
And ungalloped, ungalloped, ungalloped, ungalloped a bit:
Then I cast off my bluff-coat, let my bowler hat fall,
Took off both my boots and my trousers and all—
Drank off my stirrup-cup, felt a bit tight,
And unbridled the saddle : it still wasn't right.

. . . .

Then all I remember is, things reeling round
As I sat with my head 'twixt my ears on the ground—
For imagine my shame when they asked what I meant
And I had to confess that I'd been, gone and went
And *forgotten the news* I was bringing to Ghent,
Though I'd galloped and galloped and galloped and galloped
  and galloped
And galloped and galloped and galloped. (Had I not would
  have been galloped ?)

ENVOI

So I sprang to a taxi and shouted " To Aix ! "
And he blew on his horn and he threw off his brakes,
And all the way back till my money was spent
We rattled and rattled and rattled and rattled and rattled
And rattled and rattled—
And eventually sent a telegram.'

* * *

Time, space, ignorance and indeed Heaven forbid
that we should attempt to quote or even misquote all
the palfrey little horse-poems in the English language,
while to reproduce such Gaelic gaucheries as the poet
Burns's story of the man who went riding *in a Tam
o' Shanter* (!) would be merely Piling Tedium upon
Ossian (the man was punished by having his mare's

tail cut off by some special Scotch animals called
'cutty sharks', which was just about what he
deserved).

There are, of course, other styles, harmless in their
way but not compelling : for instance, you are not
bound to agree with the sentiments of the G. K.
Chesternut school that

> ' The Great White Horse of Blumpington
> Is the whitest horse I know.'

You personally may prefer the Great Buff Horse of
Orpington, in which case you are at perfect liberty to
state, in a blumping great ballad, that it is easily the
buffest horse in Christendom.

Nor need you ever fall, or even peck, for that
romantic but hopelessly unhorsemanlike style of
poetry which avoids technical terms at all costs, even
the word ' horse ', and bounds along in a most un-
collected manner about ' chargers ' and ' coursairs '
and, above all, ' steeds '—with the result that only a
professor of literature can tell one famous poetical
Steed from another and give you the straight tip that
John Gilpin, for instance, favoured a *nimble steed* with
a *flowing mane*, while Lord Byron's hero with the
curious Russian name of Marzepan was cruelly done
up in a parcel with a *noble steed* which (unless Byron's
Late Information was wrong) ran with a *bristling
mane*. Writing this sort of poetry is, in fact, enough
to get you warned off the Turf or even blackbald out
of the Towel Horses Improvement Society.

On the other hand, there is no need to over-bit your
Muse and sink to the plodding style which results in
your calling yourself by some pedestrian little name

such as ' *James Thomson* ' and writing pathetically
urgent little lines like—

> ' *Give a man a horse he can ride,* '

—described (wrongly) by Capt. Pontoon as ' a plaintive
but reasonable request ', and stigmatised (rightly) by
Col. Numnah-Smith as ' a piece of cowardly nonsense,
since there is no horse a man cannot ride, provided a
man has a good pair of everything and the courage to
boot it '.

In fact you cannot do better than the primitive or
' folk ' style of Horse-poetry of which *Widdicombe Fair*
is by far the best-known example.

We quote, with some misgiving, from a gramophone
record of this great poem, made by Capt. Pontoon with
a patent Home-Recorder instrument of his own
invention. Unfortunately it is one of those records
(probably familiar to you) in which *the needle keeps
getting stuck in one groove.* . . .

WIDDICOMBE FAIR

(Pontoon-Galumphia Record No. 1066)

' " Tom Pearse, Tom Pearse, lend me your gray mare,"
    (All along, down along, out along, by-with-or-from-along
     lea)
" For I want for to go, for to Widdicombe Fair,
With Bill Brewer, Bill Brewer, Bill Brewer, Bill Brewer, Bill
     Brewer, Bill Brewer, Bill Brewer . . . (*give the needle
     a shove*)
    Old oblong old Cobley and all,—
    Old wobbly old Cobley and all."

" And when shall I see again my gray mare ? "
    (All along, come along, cut along, get along for Heaven's
     sake)

" With Bill Bobbly, Will Wobbly, Dick Nobbly, Harry Tate,
    Sir John Simon, Sir Pundit Motilal Tej Bahadur,
    Bahadur, Bahadur, Bahadur, Bahadur, Bahadur . . .
    (*another little shove*)
Old Coblywob-nobly and all,—
Hobgobly-nobwobly and all."

Chorus :—With Bill Bobbly, Bill Bobbly, Bill Bobbly, Bill
    Bobbly, Bill Bobbly, Bill Bobbly, Bill Bobbly . . .
    (*O, take the thing right off*)

APPENDIX

For the benefit of those who prefer something quite
up-to-date, we should add that the passionate tender-
ness of the horseman towards the horse has inspired
one of the most heart-rending, drum-splitting New
York Negro Spirituelles of the day.

Based on the loving Horseman's care of the *Sensitive
Frog* (see p. 61), and accompanied by a full jazz
symphony orchestra of choke-bore and broken-wind
brass and wood instruments, drums, traps, buggy-
axlephones, wurlitzers and pantechnicons, it goes just
like this :—

DAT SENZERDIV' FROG

(first sung by Mr. Louis Drumstrong at the Pan-
Gongsters International Jazzboree, Chicago, 1933)
Rider !
Rider ! !

> (*soft neighing of muted trumpets, involuted fog-
> horns and reputed-pint-drench-horns*)

Rider ! ! !
Try ter
Giv'n eye ter

Dat Senzerdiv' Fraarg ! ! ! !

> (*sustained muling, puking and drooling of trombones, hambones, accordions, discordions, string-pleated bedford-cordions, etc.*)

Dâ-dâ-dâ-dâ-dâdâ-dâ . . .—

He got no 'noceros shirt !

So don' you do him no dirt ! . . .

> (*sinister crescendo or crascredo of E-flat drum-throbs, gum-sobs and Plum-flat thingummy-bobs*)

Don' hurt—Dâ-dâ-dâ-dâ—

> (*plaintive whinneying of demented oboes, stale-scented hoboes and disappointed veterinary surgeons*)

Dat Senzerdiv'—

Hart-diggety-diggety-friggety-friggety—

Fraaaaaaaarg ! ! ! ! ! ! ! !

(*Supercrash of Cymbals, timbrels, tumbrils, surcingles, frog-horns, hot-doghorns, hunting-crops, shunting-whistles, fire-engines, ambulances, Æolian-Bœotian-Vocational-Eisteddfods, etc. etc. etc. etc.*)

HOW TO WRITE ABOUT THE HORSE

II. PROSE, CONYERS, ETC.

If you are going to write in prose about the Horse at all, you had better make up your mind at once to write *about Hunting*. Because it will come to that in the end. So leu in to it ! There are two methods. You can write a novel (or could, if you happened to be able to), in which case you will require all the usual literary fal-lals—a Style and a Romantic Story, for instance (both of which you can easily borrow from some literary hack), and a Knack of describing the countryside as only a man who has hunted all his life *can* describe it—or possibly as only a man who has read other people's descriptions of the countryside probably could describe it.

The alternative is the geographical-cum-genealogical style for which you will have to know ' every inch ' of your country and every leaf on the County Family Trees, and will have to have hunted the Spottesmore Pack yourself in your great-grandfather's day, and so be qualified to contribute an article on your own ' bit-o'country ' to some colossal enclycopedantic work on Hunting in the Shires, or the 'Nineties, or wherever you happen to have got stuck.

Let us consider the novel first.

A. THE HUNTING NOVEL
(with literary fal-lals.)

These are the kind of sentences you must practise :—

" Autumn still lingered over the gladsome pastures as though loth to depart (*or, alternatively, hurried over the loathsome pastures, as though glad to depart*). In the grey wreaths of mist that hung low by the river there was promise of a hot scent for the morrow.

" ' Gad ! ' muttered Godfrey, between his teeth, striking his jodhpores savagely with the handle of his hunting-crop, as he chatted nervously with Marjory on the terrace, long after the dressing-gong had boomed resoundingly through the great hall . . . (*or, perhaps better, ' Humph ! ' muttered Humphrey between his*

*drinks, jogging Marjory's paws nervously as he boomed
savagely on the dinner-gong with the handle of his hunting-
crop.*)

" ' Gad ! (*or ' Humph !* ') If the bitches run their fox
straight and keep up-wind to-morrow, blast me if I
don't put the old walnut short-horn at Crowner's Brook
with the best of them ! '

" Marjory glowed knowingly : Godfrey (*or possibly
Gadfrey*) was so downright, so forthright, so fifth-
rate . . . (*or better, Humphrey was so upright, so
humphright, so Pontefright.*) [1] To her, the way he
shaped to-morrow would mean everything, anything,
nothing . . ."

If you go on practising this long enough, in the end
you will get it just-right, just-wrong, or, almost
certainly, justawful.

B. ENCYCLOPARENTHESIS

A TYPICAL DAY IN THE MOULDY WEDNESDY COUNTRY

And now, the parenthetical-parental non-stop
style :—

' The meet was with the Mouldy at Willoughby-in-
the-Wilds—what more could one wish for with Skirter's
Gorse to draw not two fields away ? " Skirters,"
blackthorn and privet—30 acres—and a sure draw for
a bold fox formerly the property of Sir Donald Belvoir
who sowed the first bush (? brush) in 1832 and hunted
over the Maundy Thursdy Country for 56 seasons—
was but quite recently bought by Sir Patrick

---

[1] Pronounced Pumphright, you cads.

Chestnut nephew to the late Lord Wednesdy who hunted the Spottesmore himself for ten seasons just before the war and is wont to say " Give me the Mouldy Wednesdy country for a cracking pace a cut at the open water and 90% of horseflesh stone-cold.' " (And Wottesmore he's devilishright and always Willoughby !)

'On the day in question a brace left " Skirters " down wind simultaneously. The bitches carried a good head and hunted on without dwelling to Oakley pastures a mile due west of Turnover Spinneys. The Spinneys once the property of the famous Sir Charles Dumpling (" Charley ", as old Jack latterly Viscount Turnover used to call him) who was a great supporter of foxhunting and definitely animal-minded became incorporated some ten years ago in the Spottesmore estates (as they were then) and bought up four years later by that great sportsman Sir Matthew Saturdy (as he is now) but sold two years ago to Sir Mondy Fortnight (as he soon will be) when Sir Matthew's brother Sir Absolute Mutt (as he always has been) was raised to the peerage taking the title of Lord Tuesdy-country.

'There was a slight check in Oakley . . .'

But practically no stops; the pace, pedigrees, etc., being too good.

BIT IX

DRIVING IT

' A four-in-hand is worth two in a barouche.'
Old Harness-room saying.

DRIVING the horse is practically obsolete now, but it is pleasant for us older (in fact practically obsolete) folk to look back on the days when 'buses, trams, even railway trains, were drawn by the Horse; when Queen Victoria graced the Park in her Royal Mail Coach, and my lords Tilbury, Tandem, Shandrydan and the rest used to drive down regularly to Ascot in their smart ' four-wheelers ', ' wains ' and ' bijou waggonettes ', and the wild Marquis of Kickshaw used to drive his Rickshaw irregularly into the Serpentine; when every governess had her governess-cart and lived in daily fear that the bottom would be kicked out of her little world.

For Driving the horse was not so easy as it looked: there was always the danger that the horse would kick over its braces, or get the shafts between its teeth: and there was always the possibility of driving the horse too far (say, into the billiard-room), or even of driving it mad.

The harness was difficult, too: it was not easy to conceive how the horse ever got into all those hames and terrets and blinkers and breech-blocks, and always surprising how easily it could get out of the lot, one way or another.

The great tip, we all knew, was *never to put the cart before the horse*, especially when harnessing-up, because if we did the horse guessed what was on and backed away, but to lay a trap for it very quietly behind its back and then go in front and show it the collar so that it walked backwards unwittingly into the trap (a trick invented by the first Baron Shaftsbury).

But all this, we agree, is rather dull reading for up-to-date people, and the only reason nowadays for dragging carriages into a book is to enable the artist to conceive a lot of rather jolly obsolete pictures of *Hansom-cabs* (invented by Lord Hansom, a nice-looking but cowardly nobleman who liked to get as far away from the horse as possible and steer it by faith, television, etc.) and *Broughams* (invented by Lord Brougham-and-Woa) and *Gigs* (by Phæton out of Respectability) and *Barouches* (by Baroque out of Farouche, obviously) and *brakes* and *buggies* and *sulkies* and *growlers* and *stage-coaches* and *post-chaises* and *autre-choses*, and to depict them, with all the *Diligences* at his command. . . . (See rather jolly obsolete pictures overleaf.)

BOOKS TO READ

The Noble Animal	by Col. F. le Ch. Numnah-Smith, M.F.H., V.C., D.S.O., etc.
The Blood of My Ancestors	by the same **author.**
Shires and Squires	Same.
Squires and Shires	Same again.
Shires and Shires and Squires and Squires	What's yours ?
Stallion's Reach	by Will Wisp, O.S.P. (late Head-groom to the Marquis of Headstall).
Lady into Boot	by Fr. Chalk.
Musical Rides	by Count Pointerpoint.
According to Crocker	by Crocker.
The Pastern Letters	

BOOKS NOT TO READ

Dirigible Quadrupeds	by Capt. W. D. Pontoon, M.C., B.S.A., R.E.
With Moss Bros. At Ascot	Ditto.
'Ware Squire !	

(or any other books by that unhorseworthy man)

THE END